Stories, Myths, Chants, and Songs
of the Kuna Indians

 **LLILAS Translations from Latin America Series**

Stories, Myths, Chants, and Songs of the Kuna Indians

Compiled, edited, and translated by Joel Sherzer

Illustrated by Olokwagdi de Akwanusadup

Photographs by Joel Sherzer

 University of Texas Press, Austin
Teresa Lozano Long Institute of Latin American Studies

First University of Texas Press Edition, 2003

Requests for permission to reproduce material from this work should be sent to
Permissions, University of Texas Press, P.O. Box 7819, Austin, Texas 78713-7819

♾The paper used in this publication meets the minimum requirements of American
National Standard for Information Sciences–Permanence of Paper for Printed Library
Materials, ANSI Z39.48–1984.

Library of Congress Cataloging-in-Publication Data

Stories, myths, chants, and songs of the Kuna Indians / compiled, edited, and
    translated by Joel Sherzer ; illustrated by Olokwagdi de Akwanusadup ; photographs
    by Joel Sherzer.—1st University of Texas Press ed.
        p. cm. — (LLILAS Translations from Latin America Series)
    Includes bibliographical references and index.

    ISBN 0-292-70237-X

        1. Cuna Indians—Folklore. 2. Cuna Indians—Music. 3. Cuna mythology. 4. Oral
tradition—Panama. 5. Folklore—Performance—Panama. 6. Cuna language—Texts.
I. Sherzer, Joel. II. Teresa Lozano Long Institute of Latin American Studies. III.
Series.

F1565.2.C8S77 2004
398.2'089.9783—dc22

                                                                        2003062176

A NAKUDILI
– Mi tierna canción de Amor
sonrisa de sol y luna –

Y A BURSOB
– Achiote de mi espiritu
jagua de Vida.–

Con Amor, Olo

and

To the memory of Anselmo Urrutia, close friend, collaborator,
and deep fountain of knowledge.

With fond and everlasting remembrance,
Joel

Contents

Chapter 1. Introduction 1

Part I. Humorous and Moralistic Stories

Chapter 2. *The One-Eyed Grandmother*
Told by Pedro Arias 13

Chapter 3. *The One-Eyed Grandmother*
Written and read by Hortenciano Martínez 47

Chapter 4. *The Turtle Story*
Told by Chief Nipakkinya 59

Chapter 5. *The Way of the Turtle*
Told by Pedro Arias 71

Part II. Myths and Magical Chants

Chapter 6. *Counsel to the Way of the Devil Medicine*
Performed by Anselmo Urrutia 83

Chapter 7. *The Way of Cooling Off*
Performed by Pranki Pilos 91

Chapter 8. *The Way of the Rattlesnake*
Performed by Olowiktinappi 129

Chapter 9. *The Way of Making Chicha*
Performed by Mastaletat 147

Chapter 10. *The Way of the Sea Turtle*
Performed by Tiowilikinya 191

Part III. Women's Songs

Chapter 11.   *Chicha Song*
              Performed by Justina Pineda Castrellan   213

Chapter 12.   *Three Kuna Lullabies*
              Performed by Julieta Quijano, Brieta Quijano,
              and Donalda Garcia   223

Chapter 13.   *Counsel to a Parakeet*
              Performed by Justina Pineda Castrellan   237

Notes   241

References   245

Index   247

List of Illustrations

by Olokwagdi de Akwanusadup

1. Young girl making a mola   xii
2. Boy sees house in the distance   9
3. Grandmother splashing in hot water   12
4. Dog licks boy back to life   17
5. King of village presents his daughter to boy   46
6. Boy directs dog to attack ogre   49
7. Jaguar and Turtle exhausted after race   58
8. Jaguar and Turtle shake hands   63
9. Monkey punches Turtle in the chest   70
10. Turtle hits Monkey with a stick   73
11. Counseling the way of the devil medicine   82
12. Counseling the cooling off spirits   90
13. Chanting to the chicha   95
14. Hunting a dangerous snake   128
15. Kuna man competes at drinking chicha with his wife   135
16. Women drinking chicha during puberty festivities   146
17. Machi Esakunappi on the beach watching his wives in the sea   190
18. Women ritually drinking chicha during puberty festivities   212
19. Young girl hanging clothes on a line   222
20. Young boy fishing off a Kuna dock   225
21. Parakeet on dock overlooks the sea   236

List of Photographs

by Joel Sherzer (photo section follows page 125)

1. Pedro Arias speaking in the Mulatuppu gathering house
2. Hortenciano Martínez writing in a notebook
3. Chief Nipakkinya watching a sporting event
4. Anselmo Urrutia working with a tape recorder
5. Pranki Pilos wearing his medicinal specialist's clothing and carrying his staff
6. Olowiktinappi gathering medicine in the jungle
7. Olowiktinappi making a basket
8. Olowiktinappi performing *The Way of the Rattlesnake*
9. Chief Mastaletat
10. Woman grinding sugarcane to make chicha
11. Men grinding sugarcane to make chicha
12. Chicha in pots
13. Men stirring chicha
14. Chicha fermenting
15. Pedro Arias sitting in front of fermented chicha
16. Kantule Ernesto Linares and his assistant, Andrew García, performing during puberty rites
17. Meristante Díaz and Rogelio Robles playing long flutes during puberty festivities
18. Women preparing ritual meal for puberty festivities
19. Women eating ritual meal during puberty festivities
20. Men eating ritual meal during puberty festivities
21. Jerónimo Green and Alfredo Martínez preparing hammock for puberty festivities
22. The island/village of Mulatuppu
23. Tiowilikinya
24. Juliana Quijano dressed for puberty festivities
25. Women at puberty festivities
26. Woman at puberty festivities
27. Women at puberty festivities
28. Benilda Quijano with baby

Stories, Myths, Chants, and Songs
of the Kuna Indians

Figure 1. Young girl making a mola

Chapter 1

Introduction

The performances, translations, illustrations, and photographs in this book document and display the linguistic, cultural, social, literary, and individual imagination and creativity of the oral literature of the Kuna Indians of Panama. They are intended to guide readers into an appreciation of Kuna history, philosophy, mythology, symbolism, curing practices, knowledge of plant, animal, and marine ecology, gender relations, everyday interactions and preoccupations, and especially the rhythms and aesthetics of Kuna verbal practices.

The Kuna Indians, probably best known for their molas—colorful appliqué and reverse appliqué blouses made and worn by Kuna women and sold all over the world—are one of the largest indigenous groups in the South American tropics. About 70,000 Kuna inhabit Kuna Yala, a string of island and mainland villages stretching along the Caribbean coast from near Colón to the Panama-Colombia border. In addition approximately 19,000 Kuna live in Panama City. Readers of this book have probably seen pictures of Kuna women wearing colorful molas, along with tropical beaches, in advertisements aimed at attracting tourists to Panama or Latin America more generally.

A book on Kuna literature is most appropriate for a series focusing on Latin American translations. The verbal performances presented and translated here are representative of the beauty, complexity, and diversity of the oral literary traditions of the indigenous peoples of Latin America. While appreciated by indigenous peoples themselves as oral performances, they are not readily available to western audiences in either print or audio form.[1]

Kuna literature is intimately linked to the social and cultural contexts in which it is performed. These include the gathering house, where myths are chanted, counsel is given, political speeches are made, humorous and moralistic stories are told, and people congregate at leisure times to talk and joke; the chicha house, where fermented drinks for young girls' puberty rites are made and consumed and where ritual chants for these rites are performed; and private homes where curing chants are performed for sick individuals, and lullabies, for babies.

This book is organized into three sections, I: humorous and moralistic stories; II: myths and magical chants; and III: women's songs. Humorous and moralistic stories can often be traced to European and sometimes African origins. It is possible that not only particular stories but the entire genre of storytelling was borrowed from Europeans, in particular, Spaniards, and diffused among indigenous groups, who are known to have traveled and continue to travel widely and learn each other's languages and traditions.[2] In this regard it is interesting that the Kuna use the word *kwento* (from the Spanish *cuento*) for story, one of the few Spanish words to have entered the traditional Kuna vocabulary. In spite of their origins, these stories have, over time, become very Kuna in content, style, and performance. It is fascinating how borrowed characters, themes, and motifs become incorporated into Kuna modes of being, thinking, and talking. These stories describe the Kuna environment, Kuna behavior and philosophy, and Kuna morality. Their literary properties, in particular, the way in which they are told, are quintessentially Kuna.

Myths and magical chants are addressed to representatives of the spirit world, to cure a sick patient, control evil spirits, counsel helpful spirits, or achieve a specific goal, such as protection against dangerous snakes, a successful hunt, or the preparation of the fermented drink, chicha, which is consumed at girls' puberty rites. There are also chants performed for the pleasure and amusement of both spirits and humans.

The most commonly heard women's song is the lullaby, performed by all women, from young girls to grandmothers. Women also perform magical or semi-magical chants to spirits, as well as humorous songs at girls' puberty rites.

While these three types of Kuna literature are quite different from one another, they share features that are characteristic of Kuna literature as a whole. These include extensive repetition and parallelism, especially in curing and other ritual chants; metaphorical, figurative, and esoteric vocabulary; beautiful descriptions of tropical forest and marine ecology; detailed narrations of human, animal, and spirit behavior; and play and humor. Repetition for the Kuna, as for most Latin American indigenous groups, is not negative, but is valued, appreciated, and expected aesthetically. Similarly, detailed descriptions, play, and humor are all important components of Kuna aesthetics. The Kuna love their literature, appreci-

ating it for its aesthetic as well as its social, cultural, and magical efficacy. They never tire of sitting and listening to these performances, often for hours at a time.

As is the case in many indigenous societies in the South American tropics, Kuna oral literature is often chanted or sung. Chants are usually more
esoteric and difficult for ordinary Kuna to understand than spoken
speech. Nonetheless, they are appreciated for their beauty in performance
and powerful expression of Kuna beliefs and practices.

There are certain themes that are expressed in the texts presented here,
themes that Kuna literature shares with the literatures of other indigenous
groups in Latin America. Local ecology is a central one. Plants and trees
and their magical and curative power are described in detail. These texts
display a remarkable knowledge of both plants and animals, their form,
shape, characteristics, and values. Animal behaviors and foibles are fo-
cused on, as are those of humans and spirits. In fact, the fascinating relationship that exists among the worlds of humans, animals, and spirits
in the Kuna belief system emerges in these texts. Trickster stories in particular not only illustrate the Kuna's keen observation of the animals
around them, but also communicate about social relations, including
unequal ones.

The personalities and behaviors of animals and spirits are a mirror
image and expression of Kuna human conduct. Spirits are a very important aspect of the Kuna world, in curing, magic, aesthetics, and everyday life. In these texts we see Kuna actors, human, animal, and spirit, as
wily and clever, serious and humorous, all very important traits in their
struggles against powerful forces, whether these are evil spirits or out-
siders trying to take Kuna land. As part of the description of the behavior of humans, animals, and spirits, conversations are crucial. And the
conversations depicted in these texts are wonderful renderings of those
found in everyday Kuna life.

Several of these texts deal with various aspects of young girls' puberty
rites. These include the preparation of the fermented drink, chicha, which
is consumed in great quantities during the ritual; the special bathing and
other activities individuals carry out before the ritual; and the various
activities, including competitive drinking, that go on during the ritual.

Another recurrent theme in these texts is gender relations and the roles
and worlds of women. The texts express a range and variety of gender
relations and portrayals of women, from subservient to men to strong,
willful, and confident actors. In their relations with husbands, children,
and one another, women are depicted sometimes positively, sometimes
negatively.

Finally, these stories, myths, and chants, like the Kuna life that they reflect and re-create, display considerable play and humor, as they mingle ancient legacies of indigenous Latin America with European motifs and everyday Kuna beliefs and behaviors.

The texts in this book provide a demonstration of how the Kuna understand and unify the ecological, social, cultural, and supernatural aspects of their lives through their language. Language is central and radiates out into the geographic, biological, botanical, zoological, and cultural worlds that speakers and listeners inhabit.

These texts constitute an autodescription and autoestimation of the Kuna world—Kuna social, cultural, and daily life the way the Kuna perceive it. The Kuna feel that their future as well as their past are expressed in these myths, stories, chants, and songs, which are both simple and profound, reflections of tradition as well as models for times to come. They are a legacy of the, unfortunately, vanishing verbal treasures of Latin America. They contain a learned expression of the knowledge and aesthetics of elders and ritual specialists and the sentiments of all Kuna, men, women, and children, who can understand, enjoy, and learn them.

REPRESENTATION AND TRANSLATION

The texts in this book are representations and translations of oral performances that I recorded. The rhythms of these performances, including volume, intonation, tempo, and pause pattern, are essential aspects of their aesthetics. My representations of these performances on the printed pages of this book aim at rendering their oral qualities for readers. Following current convention in the representation of indigenous American literature, including that of the Kuna, I present these texts in the form of poetic lines. I have determined lines according to pauses coupled with falling pitch, in spoken speech; according to musical pattern (a combination of pitch, tempo, and volume), as well as pause, in chants. Lines are also marked by an elaborate set of words, phrases, and affixes. Lines end with a period, and runover lines are indented. Long pauses without falling pitch are transcribed as blank spaces between words within lines. Short, interlinear pauses are represented with a comma. The line organization of the translation is identical to that of the representation of the original Kuna performance. Other expressive devices represented in the texts and translations are lengthening of sounds (indicated by doubling of letters), loud speech (indicated by capital letters), and stretched out pronunciation (indicated by dashes between syllables). Other features of the voice are indicated in parentheses.

Word boundaries in this polysynthetic language, in which there is a tendency for independent words to be shortened and affixed to other words, and in which there is not a tradition of writing, pose a particularly difficult problem. I have determined word boundaries by a combination of phonetic/phonological, grammatical, and semantic principles.

Translation, in particular from an indigenous Latin American language like Kuna into a western language like English, requires a combination of linguistic, anthropological, and literary perspectives. It involves grammar and words, knowledge of local ecology, and social and cultural concepts. I intend the translations to reflect the poetic and rhetorical subtleties, the symbolism, the allusions and presuppositions, the play and humor, and the aesthetic sensibilities of Kuna verbal life, and at the same time be understandable and appreciated by non-Kuna as they read them. More particularly, translation from Kuna oral performances to written English involves a number of issues.[3] To the degree possible, I aim at rendering the oral features of Kuna voices into written English as I do into written Kuna. These include line breaks and spaces to indicate pauses and representations of shifts in tempo and volume, as well as other dramatizations of the voice.

Kuna words consist of several suffixes following a root or stem. Verb suffixation is particularly complicated and is where much of the meaning of sentences is located. In English, syntactic patterning, including word order, plays a much greater role than in Kuna. The Kuna tense-aspect system, marked by combinations of verbal suffixes, is quite different from English. Much attention is paid to details of direction and movement, positions of actors, and timing of events. In order to retain the Kuna system as faithfully as possible, my translation at times focuses more on aspect than on tense. Native English readers occasionally may be surprised by a seeming shifting in and out of particular time frames and by sudden alterations in point of view. They will be faced with and, one hopes, appreciate an aesthetics of time very different from what they are accustomed to.

In order to remain as faithful as possible to the original Kuna, my translations are relatively literal. In addition to direction, movement, motion, position, and timing, I translate literally the set of words and phrases that play a major role in the poetic marking of lines and verses—"then," "well," "thus," "so," "therefore," "say," "see," "hear," and variations and combinations of them. These punctuate and adorn Kuna performances and my English translations of them. These are poetic as well as incantatory units. They embellish performances and are essential to their rhythm.

The common Kuna practice of quoting oneself and others is not consistently marked by expressive features in oral performances. Following western orthographic tradition, I use quotation marks whenever a speaker quotes another or herself or himself.

Kuna vocabulary is characterized by extreme variety and subtlety, reflecting and expressing the ideational, ecological, material, metaphorical, and sociolinguistic worlds of the Kuna. To the degree possible, I have translated lexical meanings, denotative and connotative, into English equivalents. Onomatopoetic words are rendered exactly as in Kuna, so as to retain the Kuna sense of sound, so essential to performance.

The individuals whose performances are represented and translated here are or were acknowledged verbal artists in their community and in several cases ritual and political leaders. They are or were friends of mine and honored me in their willingness to perform for a tape recorder. They were very proud of their knowledge and reputation and wanted this knowledge valorized by having their voices heard and read by others. I have played recordings of these performances to Kuna men and women over the years. They are greatly appreciated. In the case of young people who have never heard them performed, the recordings bring tears to their eyes.

The drawings that illustrate these texts were done by Olokwagdi de Akwanusadup, a Kuna artist well known in Panama and Central America more generally for his drawings, book illustrations, paintings, and murals. He is particularly loved by Kuna who know his wonderful illustrations of books for both adults and children, dealing with various aspects of Kuna life. His illustrations are imaginative, poetic, inspirational, political, and humorous. He listened to the recordings and read the texts and then created the illustrations included here. These illustrations are visual renderings of the Kuna imagination of their actual, mythical, mystical, and philosophical worlds. They present, with remarkable perspicacity, aspects of Kuna history, ecology, and cultural artifacts, human and animal gestures and personalities, and dress, in ways that are both stylized and realistic, with extreme sensitivity and elegance.

Also accompanying the texts are photographs I took of the performers and the activities they describe. These photographs show people's faces, gestures, activities, and engagement in performance. They are intended to enliven the texts and provide a sense of being present at Kuna verbal performances. The illustrations and photographs also provide a perspective on the relationship between Kuna verbal and visual arts. Readers are thus presented with several intersecting renderings of Kuna literature—texts and translations of actual performances, artistic illustrations, and photographs. With the additional advantage of being able to listen to the performances on the AILLA (Archive of the Indigenous Languages of Latin America) website, they are provided with an extremely rich contextualization. Those familiar with Kuna molas are rewarded with still another aesthetic perspective on the Kuna worlds presented in the texts in this book.[4]

While the Kuna are global citizens, one of the best-known indigenous groups in Latin America, they speak a minority language and possess and perform an endangered oral literature. Their stories, myths, chants, and songs invoke and express intimate knowledge of the world at multiple levels, and a remarkable aesthetics. The texts in this book provide an opportunity for the unique and eloquent voices of an extraordinary people to be seen and heard.

ORTHOGRAPHY

The Kuna language is transcribed here in one of the several alphabets that have been used for it.[5] There are five vowels, as in Spanish:

a: *nate* "he/she went"
e: *eye* "yes"
i: *misi* "cat"
o: *moe* "squash"
u: *ulu* "canoe"

These can be short or long (doubled): *tii* "water," *muu* "grandmother," *kaa* "hot pepper." Each vowel counts as a single syllable. Stress is usually on the penultimate syllable.

There are four stop consonants, which can be either voiced or voiceless. The voiced consonants are represented as follows:

p (pronounced b): *poe* "cry"
t (pronounced d): *tii* "water"
k (pronounced g): *kunne* "eat"
kw (pronounced gw): *korokwa* "ripe"

The voiceless stop consonants are represented as long (doubled) versions of the voiceless consonants:

pp (pronounced p): *sappi* "tree"
tt (pronounced t): *satte* "no"

kk (pronounced k): *takke* "see"
kkw (pronounced kw): *akkwe* "care for"

Nasals, liquids, and the sound r can also be short or long (doubled):

m: *ome* "woman," *mimmi* "child"
n: *nikka* "have," *sunna* "true"
l: *kwalu* "sweet potato," *kwallu* "grease"
r: *warkwen* "one"

There is a sibilant s and an affricate ch:

s: *wisi* "know"
ch: *machi* "boy"

There are two semivowels, w and y:

w: *wini* "bead"
y: *daysa* "saw"[6]

Figure 2. Boy sees house in the distance

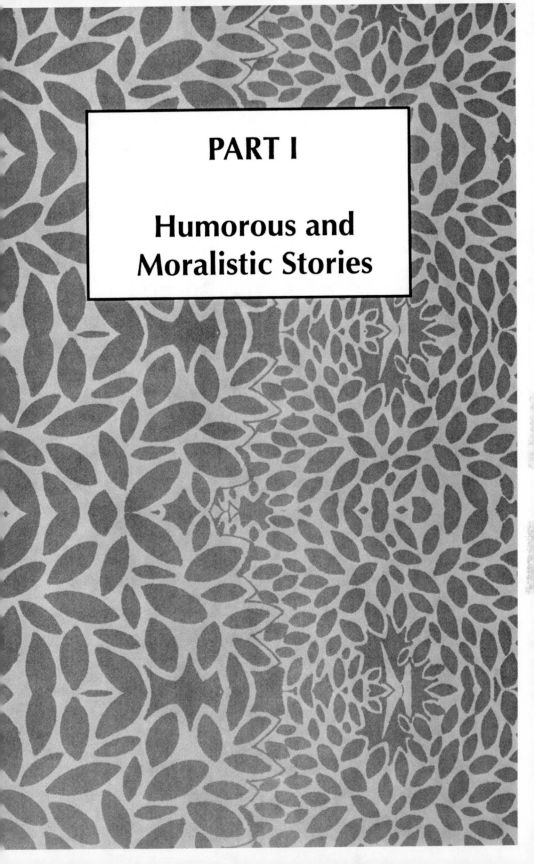

PART I

Humorous and Moralistic Stories

Figure 3. *Grandmother splashing in hot water*

Chapter 2

The One-Eyed Grandmother

Told by Pedro Arias

Muu ipya kwakkwena/The One-Eyed Grandmother was told by Pedro Arias in the gathering house of the village of Mulatuppu in Kuna Yala on June 29, 1970, on the occasion of the annual celebration of the creation of the school in the village. On such occasions the Kuna engage in both serious discourse and humorous performances. Pedro Arias was an *arkar* "chief's spokesman" and highly regarded as a good storyteller. *The One-Eyed Grandmother* is a fascinating case of European themes and motifs that somehow diffused through indigenous America to the Kuna and became combined with Kuna elements to create a very Kuna humorous and moralistic tale.

Pedro Arias's telling of *The One-Eyed Grandmother* consists of four episodes. Episodes I and II, a Kuna version of the European *Hansel and Gretel* story, describe how a father, at the urging of a new wife, purposely loses his children in the jungle and how the children find their way to a home owned by a one-eyed grandmother, who gives the story its Kuna name. The children get caught by the grandmother, who wants to eat them. But they trick her, in a miraculous series of events, and end up escaping. This episode is a kind of trickster tale, though each of the other episodes contains trickster elements as well.

In episode III, also probably of European origin, the sister falls in love with an ogre who convinces her to kill her brother. But the brother, helped by his dog, manages to kill the ogre instead. The boy then leaves his sister. In the fourth and final episode, of probable European origin as well, the boy comes upon a village that is under attack by an ogre. Again, he successfully overcomes the ogre. As a result, he wins the hand of the daughter of the king of the village in marriage, with, however, a surprising and ambiguous ending.

As European as these episodes might sound in this general overview, in Pedro's telling the story is very Kuna.[1] This includes social and cultural practices and assumptions shared by Kuna tellers and audiences. Most Kuna live on islands and travel by canoe to the jungle mainland to hunt, farm, gather medicine, wash clothes, and get fresh water from jungle rivers. The island/mainland, sea/jungle contrasts are constant features of Kuna culture, society, and ecology, and themes of Kuna literature. Doves and other birds are some of the animals the Kuna hunt in the jungle. Collared peccaries are native to the area and highly valued as game animals. The Kuna use dogs for both hunting and protection. The sugarcane husks and corn left by the children to find their way home are basic to Kuna agriculture and ritual.

The social and kinship structure depicted is clearly from a male oriented, political leader's perspective, especially that of the 1970s, when the story was recorded. Women are viewed on the one hand as fragile and in need of male protection, but on the other hand, as are people in general, as susceptible to jealousy and untrustworthiness, leading to mischievous behavior. The conflict between family loyalty and betrayal is a constant theme.

The characters in this story, like the European versions they are derived from, have no names, as distinct from magical chants, where secret, esoteric names are crucial to these chants' efficacy. These characters, the father and his new wife, the brother and sister, the grandmother, the king of the village and his daughter, and the various ogres, all have personalities, and they are Kuna personalities, including playful and not so playful tricking and love of talk and quoting others. While the Kuna demonstrably adore children, the new wife wants a new family, without the father's children from his first marriage. But the father clearly loves his children. The conflict in this matriarchal and matrilocal society is resolved in the wife's favor, and the father gets rid of his children.

While the children suffer throughout, the boy is the constant hero. He is continually tricked, by his father, sister, and others, and yet prevails on each occasion. While he is with his sister, he takes the lead in making decisions. She on the other hand gets them both into trouble and ultimately deceives her brother. The grandmother is a complex character, reflected in the network of meanings associated with the Kuna word *muu*, which include "grandmother," "old woman," and "midwife." I have chosen "grandmother" for my English translation here. Grandmothers are an important presence in Kuna homes and demonstrate loving and playful care of their grandchildren. But they are also respected and at time feared for their knowledge of tradition, which in the case of midwives, includes magic and ritual.[2] The king's daughter, offered to the boy as a reward for saving her village, is both mischievous and imagined to be deceptive by the boy. The various monsters in the story are all called *nia*, which the Kuna use to signify devil, monster, or ogre. I have translated it here as "ogre," because of the European origin of the creatures involved and their ogre-like features.[3]

The language of this story is colloquial and informal, colorful and vibrant. It is easily understood by the audience, which listens with attention, appreciates it, and laughs at humorous moments. Pedro alternates descriptive detail and moralistic and metacommunicative commentary. The story is moved along by means of directly quoted conversations between protagonists, including animals and ogres, who act and talk like humans. Miraculous events serve as turning points of the story. The children are told by a quoted letter, brought to them by a dove, how to trick the grandmother. And what follows is an exact replay of the letter. Written letters play a significant role in this oral society, which has always had great respect for literacy. The boy is revived by a dog who licks him back to life.

Pedro alternates loud and soft and fast and slow speech, giving the story its own particular rhythm. He manipulates the optional verbal suffixes of body position to highlight the actions of the characters. He repeats words for rhythmic effect and to mimic the sounds, movements, actions, and gestures in the story:

> The children went along placing placing placing placing placing
>   placing the ashes (gets softer) along they went.
> When the water is boiling, boiling, boiling, boiling
> The dog licks licks licks licks licks licks licks licks (gets softer)
>   he did only that.
> He did only that, the dog was licking him, licking licking.

And he makes use of the rich set of Kuna onomatopoetic words for expressive purposes:

> The rain came down strong *suu*.
> And the boy is standing taking it away *ikkír*.
> Well as it passed   at that moment the girl was heard ah, when
>   she laughed ye ye ye ye.
> The grandmother got angry, she STOOD UP the grandmother
>   did *piiir*.
> She did it *MOK*.

In addition to its content, the context of the telling of *The One-Eyed Grandmother* is particularly Kuna. It occurs in the gathering house, which is the setting for political meetings as well as entertainment. Pedro Arias uses the occasion to be both humorous and moralistic. He tells the story to visiting anthropologist and linguist Joel Sherzer, throwing in one or two Spanish and English words to highlight humor, and asking me questions as he would a Kuna *apinsuet* "responder." But he interjects a very Kuna moral, about caring for others, competition and jealousies among people, including family members, and not giving people credit for their achievements. He stresses at the end of his telling that *The One-Eyed Grandmother* is a serious Kuna story and states, in conventional Kuna fashion, that it is much longer than the version he has just told.

Olokwagdi de Akwanusadup's illustrations reflect Pedro's telling of the story as well as his own view of it. Olokwagdi selected four significant moments in Pedro's story and translated them visually in his own imaginative way. In figure 2, the boy, the dominant figure, is high up in a tree above the jungle canopy, and sees smoke coming from the grandmother's house in the distance. The boy has long hair and wears only a cloth skirt, quite possibly the way Kuna men dressed before they switched to a more western style.[4] The sister seems very small standing below looking up at her brother. The distant house is unmistakably Kuna, with its, probably, bamboo walls and thatch roof. In figure 3, the grandmother is splashing about in the boiling water in which she is killed. She is dressed as contemporary traditional Kuna women do, including short hair, wrist and ankle beads, and a nose ring. In figure 4, while the boy is being licked back to life by his dog, his sister is walking off stealthily with a dog/ogre. The dog/ogre is human-like in dress and demeanor. The sister wears the headkerchief, skirt, and ankle beads of traditional Kuna, and goes barefoot. The scene is a typical Kuna one—canoes moored on the beach and placed on poles, and a bamboo house with thatch roof. In figure 5, in the village that is the setting for the final scene of the story, both men and women are dressed in the traditional Kuna way, the women contemporary, and the men as Olokwagdi imagines them to have done. Two of the men are involved in serious conversation, while other men and women listen.

My photograph (photo 1) shows Pedro Arias standing in the Mulatuppu gathering house making a speech.

Here is the story, in both Kuna and English.

Figure 4. Dog licks boy back to life

Kuna

Episode I. The man gets rid of his two children

takkarku   emi machi machi tayleku kamaitii   ome, purkwichursi a.
ome purkwis.
ome purkwisku, mimmikana nikka, warpo.
machikwa, punolo.
tey nikkaku, taytisunna, mimmi, tunkutani punolo tii susukwati.   5
teki ipakwenki, papteka, mimmi takkerpat a.
ei mimmi warpo appin na pek an sokku yer takke, tey taitisunna.

tek ipakwenki taylearku, pap ome apeali a.
ome nikku soke.
napir soke a.   10
papte ome nikkupierpat.
ome moka, "pe an nikkupi?" soke kar soke a.
eye an pe nikkuo napir soke a.
tey na ome nikkuchunto papa.
kep ome nikkusku, kar soysunna, e machereka.   15
"pe mimmi warpo we tiitti, pe parmitoye a.
pe mimmi pe parmito takkenye.
pe mimmi an apesurye a.
pe mimmi pe parmisale, kep anmar na yarpa, na, kumalo takken.
ittosa.   20
na yarpa vivir kumalo, ittos nuekwa.
nuekwa anmar kapoye.
pe mimmi weki an apesurye."
machere soysunna "napir, tekirti pane an mimmi an   sappurpa
    perpenaoye a.

mimmikwate yaipa kutani, pirka pikwa nikka?"   25
mimmi pinsatimosunna.
napir.
kep pap ka sokkali   "pane   mimmiye   nu aminamarkoloye a."
natsunto.
montanya, ittos, nate.   30
untar yala pirri, natetkine, mimmika soysunna.
"wek pe an etarpemaloye.

English

Episode I. *The man gets rid of his two children*

Thus   now this man this man indeed is going about   since his wife,
    had died ah.
His wife had died.
When his wife died, he had two, children.
A boy, and a girl.
Well he is seeing, those he has, the children, growing up the girl is there
    and the boy.   5
Well one day, the father, he loves his children very much ah.
His two children indeed I tell you he loves very much, well it seems.

Well one day indeed, the father fell in love with a woman ah.
He gets married it is said.
It is true it is said ah.   10
And the father wants very much to get married.
The woman does also, "You want to marry me?" she says she says to
    him ah.
"Yes I will marry you" it is true it is said ah.
Well he married the woman the father did.
Then when he got married, she says to him, to her husband.   15
"Your two children who are going about here, you must get rid of
    them ah.
You must get rid of your children see.
Your children I do not want ah.
When you have sent your children away, then we will indeed be together,
    indeed, see.
Did you hear.   20
We will *vivir* together, did you hear good.
We will sleep well together.
Your children I do not want them here."
The husband says "OK, well tomorrow I will go leave   my children
    in the mountain ah.

The children are getting older, how old are they?"   25
The children are thinking also.
(Seems like children know that the father is going to send them away)
OK.
Then the father comes and says to them   "Tomorrow   children   let's
    go to get doves ah."
And they went.
To the *montaña*, did you hear, they went.   30
When they got to, the top of a hill, he says to the children.
"You must wait for me here.

emi nu namaymaye.
emi an nu aminakoloye a."
mimmikwa pechunto a.   35
mimmikwa takkarkua   emi   ka ukka sesat.
kai ukka, kai ukkate natku, urki nakusku eti, papti papsorpa nait ka
   ukka mese mese mese mese mese mese (gets softer), eti natsursi ittos
   kai ukka.

yar piri moskusku.
kepe, "nu namaymai" kar sokku, mimmi pesat, papti nate.
kep papti itu arsunto, PIIIIR.   40
mimmi tey mellet.
e susu pokwa.
taimar oet, punolo oete.
takkarku, pia nate?
"pap oet."   45
wepa sus sokkuti.
"pap an itu natmalatteye a."
teysokku, ka ukka maitpa takoye.
wepa noniku, ome itu sii taynonisunto.
kep wepa kar soysunna, "em pia   emi pe machi pe perpeap" soke. 50
"pe mimmi" "eye" soke, "an mimmi an mette ar takkenye."
"a nuet" takken soke.
ome kar soke, "wek an apeye."
asapin ome asapin maskunpuysunto, ome si machere maskunsi.
mimmiti, ka ukkapa alit.   55
peekwatse, imas nue maskunsi mimmi kornonisunto a.
nekase.
"anna papye," kar soke a, "papye."
takkarku papa mmm, ome nuuu.
"pe mimmi pe perpeapsur" sokeye ka soke.   60
"pia pe mimmi taniye?"
sursoke "pia tanitipa?" soke a.
"tekir pan perpenaparsunno takken."
"aye.
pan pe operpenao takken" kar soke.   65

Now the dove that is lying singing there.
Now I'm going to go and get the dove ah."
The children stayed behind ah.   35
The children thus   now   took along sugarcane husks.
With sugarcane husks, with sugarcane husks when they started off, in the
    boat when they started off, and the father behind the father they were
    going along putting putting putting putting putting putting (gets
    softer) sugarcane husks, as they went did you hear sugarcane husks.

When they got to the top of the mountain.
Then, "The dove is lying singing" he said to them, and the children
    remained, and the father left.
Then the father returned home ahead of them, *PIIIIR*.   40
The children well they stayed.
The boy both of them.
See he was lost, the girl was lost.
So, where to go?
"Father is lost."   45
The other one the brother said.
"Since Father went ahead of us ah."
Therefore, by means of the sugarcane husk that was lying there they
    would be able to come back.
When that one (the father) got back, he came and saw his wife sitting
    there in front of him.
Then she says to him, "now where   now your son did you leave him
    there?" she says.   50
She says "Your children" "Yes" he says, "I threw away my children
    and returned home see."
"That is good" see she says.
The wife says to him, "This is what I want."
Facing one another the wife facing one another they were sitting eating,
    the wife is sitting the husband is sitting eating.
And the children, they returned home by means of the sugarcane
    husks.   55
Finally, it was done and while they are sitting eating well the children
    came and called ah.
To the house.
"Hey Father," they say to him ah, "Father."
So the father (says) "Mmm," the mother (looks) *nuuu*.
"Your children you did not leave them" she says she says to him.   60
"Where are your children coming from?"
He responds "Where could they be coming from?" he says ah.
"Well tomorrow I will go and leave them again see."
"Yes.
Tomorrow I will go and leave them for you" he says to her.   65

"pan pe perpenasulir, anse pe perkuoye."
napir soke.
pane kinpalo takken soke.

paneki, waitar, kinepali.
mimmi op kway sesa opa.   70
kep op urpe urpe urpe urpe natparsunto anpa kannarsepa, yala pirri.
kep mimmika soysunna, "wek pe an aptakkoye a.
e nu namaymapin nu aminakoloye."
patto mimmi wiskutanikusmosunna, pap e yartakket.
napir soke.   75

kep immasku   kannar piiiiir arparkua, anpa, omese taynonipa anpa,
    kannar noniparto omese a.
kep ome soysunna, "pe mimmi pe, opesa, opes" takken soke.
a napir takkenye a.
kep maskunpukkwa, mimmite op kwaypa arparsunnat, kannar.
imma, papasepa.   80
wepa kep ome uluarsunto, "peka soy takken pe mimmi pe mel, setaye,
    ipika pe mimmi pe, arta takkenye a?"
sursoke, "tekir pane an perpenapaloye a."
napir soke, "pe mimmi opeloko takkenye."
teki kep taylearku   kep panekine, mimmi kep yartaylesunnoto, purru
    sesat purru.
purru pe wisi?   85
purru e so a.

eye.
a sesat, mimmi.
natsun mimmi purru urpe urpe urpe urpe urpe urpe (gets softer) naate.
kep a mosku kep, pap ka soysunna "mimmiye weki nu namayma wey
    pe pan apinittokoye."   90
kep nate.
tey natetki eti pap aypili (unfinished word < aypilis) a, ti wiarsunto.
ti suuu.
purru yokkus.
pia partako mimmi?   95
pa punolo pia tako machikwa suli ekka pire, pire, pire. (< aypire)
ti armitku ittos, wiletsun, napir soke.
mimmi pinsasunna.
machikwa.

"If you do not go and leave them tomorrow, you have finished it for us."
It is true it is said.
Next day ready again see say.

Next day, early in the morning, ready again.
The children took along corn kernels corn.   70
Then they went along placing placing placing placing the corn again at
   the same spot, on the hill.
Then he says to the children, "Here you must wait for me ah.
The dove is lying singing again I will go and get the dove."
The children already had come to know, that Father was tricking them.
It is true it is said.   75

Well it's done   again *piiiiir* he returned home, again, he came back and
   saw his wife again, another time he returned to his wife ah.
Then his wife says, "Your children you, left them, left them" see she says.
Ah it is true see ah.
Then while they are eating, the children returned home again, by means
   of the corn kernels, another time.
It's done, they got to their father's place again.   80
That one then the wife got mad, "I tell you see your children you did
   not, take, them why do your children, keep returning home see ah?"
He responds, "Well tomorrow I will go and leave them again ah."
It is true it is said, "You will finish off your children tomorrow see."
Well then indeed   then the next day, the children then will surely be
   tricked, ashes they took along ashes.
Do you know what ashes are? (said to Joel Sherzer)   85
The fire of the ashes ah. (an explanation for Joel Sherzer, signifying
   probably that ashes come from fire)

Yes.
That is what they took along, the children.
The children went along placing placing placing placing placing placing
   the ashes (gets softer) along they went.
Then having arrived there then, the father says to them "Children here
   the dove is lying singing here you must wait for me."   90
Then he left.
Well along the way he the father turned back ah, and it started to rain.
The rain came down strong *suu*.
The ashes disappeared.
Where could the children go?   95
And the girl where to go and the boy always in the same place turning
   around, turning around, turning around.
When the rain stopped did you hear, they got sad, it is true it is said.
The boy thinks.
The boy.

punka soysunna.   100
"emi anmar tayleku ikar pal an amiosurmarye a.
teysokku, punye peka nipa, ney takkoloye, ittosa."
suar kwichit.
suarki nakkwichunto, nipa TUkku.
nipa attaytesunna, wekittipa, wa puppurmaysi, takken soke a.   105
we inik ney sin taye a.
a inik namaloye, kep arsunto pina pina, aitenoniku a.
punka soysunna, "we inik anmar naoye.
we inik wa puppurmaysi an tas takkenye."
kep alimarsunto.   110
m.
papti pat, nonisunnat a.
pap noniku ome kar soysa "emite an mimmi, an opes an opes takken a."
napir soke.
inso mimmi yokkuchunna a.   115
kep ome na nue nikkucun ittos.
napir.

Episode II. The two children and the one-eyed woman

mimmikwa   tey wiletanisunto, peche immmaysa, tatamar nate.
mimmi nononi takkenye, ney siitse.
ney siit mosku, takkarku, muu   emi, sin tipyesii taynoni takken
     soke a.   120
mu takkar ipya kwakKWENna, naylik.
tey wepa tayleku   sus pinsakwichunna, punka soysunna a.
"emi mu sii takkenye   punorye, wey pe pan etarpoye.
an peka sin tipyalet sukoloye, anmar ukku mata kusatteye a."
kep wepa taylearku, mute ipya kwakkwena sokku weki ipya
     kwakkwennakwa weki
a.   125
weki ipya kwakkwenakwachik.
sin tipyalet sustaet ikkír.
sin tipyalet urpemait patte yaki.
machikwati sukwichit ikkír.
wep attaytakoet, sin tipyalet satte.   130
mis kamaiti mis.
mis pipoletakoto a.

Says to his sister.   100
"Now we indeed will no longer find the way ah.
Therefore, Sister I will look about for you, above, did you hear."
There is a tree standing there.
He climbed up the tree, right to the TOP.
Above he began to observe, around here, maybe there is smoke rising
    up, see say ah.   105
In this direction there must be a house ah.
In that direction they must go, then they went there slowly slowly, after
    he came down ah.
He says to his sister, "In this direction we will go.
In this direction the smoke is rising up I saw see."
Well they went.   110
m.
And the father he already, came home ah.
When the father came home he said to his wife "Now my children, I left
    them I left them see ah."
It is true it is said.
Therefore the children disappeared ah.   115
Then they (the man and the woman) got married did you hear.
It is true.

Episode II. The two children and the one-eyed woman

The children   well they were coming along suffering, a looong time
    passed, the sun disappeared.
The children came and entered see, a house that was there.
When they got to the house that was there, so, they came and saw
    now, a grandmother sitting frying pork see say ah.   120
The grandmother indeed had ONLY ONE eye, on one side.
Well that one indeed   the boy is standing there thinking, he says to his
    sister ah.
"Now there is a grandmother sitting there see   Sister, you you'll wait
    for me here.
I will go and get pork rind for you, because we are very hungry ah."
Well that one indeed, the grandmother had one eye say here only one
    eye here ah.   125
Here she had an eye on one side only.
He keeps taking the pork rind away he does *ikkír* (Kuna expression of
    movement away).
She is putting the pork rind inside the plate.
And the boy is standing taking it away *ikkír*.
That one (the grandmother) would come to observe, that there was
    no pork rind.   130
There was a cat going about there a cat.
The cat is going to get hit ah.

"mis perpe tayle sin tipyalet kunti" soke.
mis kalet saten saten saten.
suli, tule pait ipe attursakwichit sus a.   135
teki attursati, attursatii   kep punse natsunto a.
puna.
aaii pun ukkut kin mokat sin tipyalet kunne kunne kunne kunne (gets
     softer).
tey wepa pun sokkarsunna.
"susye, an sunnat an sunamokoye a."   140
sus kar soysunna.
"pe sunnat nater pe alletako" sursokeye a.
sursoke "ipika an alletako?" takken soke a.
"an ukku mesti mokatteye a."
sursoke.   145
"pe allisaletteye ittosa
mu pinna kuarta" sokeye.
"sin tipyalet kwakwen surkusar.
pinnasur kuarta takkenye.
achu   mis pipoleartaette.   150
pe allisar takkenye."
punor soke "sur an allosurye."
napir soke.

kep punor   armosunto a.
mu sus napa kwiskunonisunna.   155
kep inso mute, sin tipyalet imakko patteki urpoet urpis.
kep pinale, ipya kwakkwena sokku, kep pinale naylik suo sus ikkír.
sin tipyalet urpialir.
satte tayta koto, pule mu kuartae a.
punolo allepie kaya mok mmm (mumbling noise).   160
allepiet kaya mok (makes noise with mouth).
tey nai   nappisa punolo ittolesa a, alliarku ye ye ye ye.
mu pule kuali, oKWICHIali mu piiir.
sa MOK.
"pani sana nuekan tayleye" ka soysunna, panse tanimar panse san
     nuekan panse nonimar takkenye."   165
nuekwa etuchunnat.
ka sin tipyalet mie mie mie mie mie (gets softer) aaa purwikan ittosuli a.
ukkut matamalat ittosa.
sin akkwilemaiyop akkwilear ittolesunto ittos.

"It's the cat see who is eating the pork rind" she says.

The cat was grabbed it was it was it was.

But no, it is someone else who is standing stealing her stuff it is the
  boy ah.   135

Well he is robbing, he is robbing   then he went to his sister ah.

The sister.

Aaii since the girl is also hungry she eats eats eats eats (gets softer) the
  pork rind.

Well this one the sister says.

"Brother, by myself I will go and get it too ah."   140

The brother says to her.

"If you go yourself you will come to laugh" he responds ah.

She responds "Why will I come to laugh?" see she says ah.

"Since I am also hungry ah."

She responds.   145

"If you laugh did you hear.

The grandmother will get mad" he says.

"If one pork rind is missing.

She will get really mad see.

If the dog   if the cat is struck.   150

If you laugh see."

The sister says "No I will not laugh."

It is true it is said.

Then the girl   also went ah.

The grandmother came and stood beside the boy.   155

Then therefore the grandmother, when she would make pork rind she
  would leave them in the plate she left them.

Then slowly, from the one-eyed one say, then slowly from her one the
  boy would take it away *ikkír*.

When she came to leave the pork rind.

There was nothing see empty, the grandmother got angry ah.

The girl wants to laugh she holds her mouth *mok* mmm (mumbling
  noise).   160

She wants to laugh she holds her mouth *mok* (makes noise with mouth).

Well as it passed   at that moment the girl was heard ah, when she
  laughed ye ye ye ye.

The grandmother got angry, she STOOD UP the grandmother did *piiir*.

She did it *MOK*.

"You are good meat for me see" she says to them, "you are coming
  to me you are good meat for me you came to me see."   165

She put them close together.

She throws them throws throws throws throws (gets softer) pork rind
  aaah the little ones feel content ah.

They were very hungry.

She took care of them like one takes care of a pig it seemed did you hear.

mimmimar nue maskunmai.   170
nue tayleku   nilapa, nue nilaka uylemasunnat a.
tey nanati, nanati, nanati (gets softer).
pechekusku   untarkusku wepa mu soysunna.
"anna, pule pani wartummakan kusmartipaye a.
anse kono oyokoye.   175
kono oyotako kono warpurwisulir pe ipyoko" soket.
sus tayleku, nusa punnu amisto, nusa punnu.
nusate tani takkali sus kasat mok.
e punnu itii.
sus pinsaet niy pe ittosursi a.   180
tey taylearku, mu kep kornonisunna.
"emi taylearku, anse kono oyomar takken, sunna ani pe
      wartummakumarye."
kep sus e konoyop imachun nusa punnu oyochun weki a.
"pani ampa karra, karra karramar tayle" kar soysun, sin tipyalet kattik
      kar mie mie mie mie mie.
a ittosuli, maskunnanait punormarte a.   185
suste ittos.
tey nai tek kuti tek (gets softer), teki wepa kep punor sokkarsunna.
"susye, nusa punnuki an totopie a.
nusa punnuki an totopi takkenye."
"sur" ka sokku sus.   190
"nusa punnuki pe totoalir (end of word barely audible) pe oealirye.
pe oelesar anmar purkoetteye a."
punor sokku "sus an oeko" sokeye a.
napir soke.

tek ipakwenki, kep, punkala nusu punnu uysasunto, nusa punnuki
      totoe.   195
man nusa punnu oete.
punorse ululearto, "emi anmar pela takkenye, emi oesye emi ipi par
      oyomaloye a?"
kep aki kep   kep ekiciarsunna, "anna   pani pule wartummakusmala,
      an takke anse kono oyo."
takkarku ipi par pe oyokoe?
nusa punnu oelesat, kono oyo taylearsunto a.   200
e (Pedro says to someone else).
kono oyolearku, "a pani wartummakan kusmar tayle" soke a.

The children are eating well. 170
Good indeed   fried banana, they are being given much fried banana ah.
Well time goes by time went by time went by (gets softer).
After much time   finally that one the grandmother says.
"Let's see, how fat you have become ah?
Show me your fingers. 175
You must show your fingers if your fingers are really fat I will smash
    you" she says.
The brother indeed, got the tail of a rat, the tail of a rat.
This rat had come see and the brother grabbed it *mok.*
He took off the tail.
The brother was intelligent do you hear ah. 180
Well indeed, the grandmother then came and called to them.
"Now indeed, show me your fingers see, in truth how fat you have
    gotten for me."
Then the brother as if he were doing it with his finger showed the rat's
    tail here ah.
"You are still thin, thin real thin see" she says to them, and throws them
    throws throws throws throws more pork rind.
They are content, they keep eating the girl does ah. 185
And the boy did you hear.
Well that is how it was well (gets softer), well this one the sister then
    said.
"Brother, I want to play with the rat's tail ah.
I want to play with the rat's tail see."
"No" the brother said to her. 190
"If you play with the rat's tail (end of word barely audible) if you
    come to lose it.
If you lose it we will surely die ah."
The sister said "Brother, how will I lose it" she says ah.
It is true it is said.

Well one day, then, he gave the rat's tail to his sister, so that she would
    play with the rat's tail. 195
And she lost the rat's tail.
And he got mad at his sister, "Now we are finished see, now you lost it
    now what will we show her again ah?"
Then she (the grandmother) then   then asked "Hey there   how fat
    have you gotten, let me see your fingers show me."
Indeed what could you show again?
The rat's tail having been lost, they had to show their fingers ah. 200
e (Pedro says to someone else).
When their fingers were shown, "Ah you have become fat for me see"
    she says ah.

"a (short laugh) pani kunneti kinmarye" kar soytesunto ittos.
kep sus sokkarsunna "pe taysa soke" punka soysunto.
"wek an peka sosye.
mer pe nusa punnu oeye.   205
emite nusa punnu oes, emi takke anmar perkuo" takken soysunto a.
"anmar unnila muse perkumalo" takkenye.

soy takken soke.
napir.
teki kep tayleku ipakwenki muu, na, susu machikwa ono onochunto
     a.   210
putu.
kep kar sokkarsunna.
"emi napir" takken soke a.
"mimmimarye   emi panka tayleku   emi ti aminamalo" takken soke
     a.
"sappan pe pisnamarpaloye a.   215
sappan pe aminaoye.
tii pe aminapaloye a."
wepa sokku   "napir" soke a.
tii perpekwichunna, punor.
suste sappan amikwismoka a.   220
kep wepa sus sokkarsunna   "emi punorye anmar perkuo takkenye a.
anmar tukkin, naki aypinmalo iki na kumalotipaye?"

kar soysunto a.
susti ittosuli.
punor ittosuli.   225
esmet tummat siit.
aki, tii enolenait.
tii enolenait.
kep ipakwenki nu kukkunoni takken soke a.
nu puuuur, tik.   230

takkarku   nu yeeer (said slowly and expressively) tayle takken soke a.
nu nuekwat takkar karta nai soysun naimaliki.
karta attinna.
nu tokenoni kachunto mok.
kep pinale karta esicunto kep, suste karta wis ittolesunto.   235
sus karta apsoarsunto.
"napir" kar soke a.

"emi an peka soko takkenye a.

Ah (short laugh) "you are ready for me to eat " she said to them did you
    hear.
Then the brother said "You saw say" he said to his sister.
"I told you this.
Don't lose the rat's tail.   205
Now you lost the rat's tail, now see we will be finished" see he said ah.
"We will be finished off by the grandmother" see.

He says see he says.
It is true.
Well then indeed one day the grandmother, indeed, had the brother the
    boy show show her (his finger) ah.   210
Out *putu*.
Then she says to them.
"Now it is true" see she says ah.
"Children   now you for me indeed   now will go and get water" see
    she says ah.
"And you will go and cut firewood ah.   215
You will go and get firewood.
And you will go and get water ah."
They said   "Alright" they say ah.
She is standing carrying the water, the sister is.
And the brother is standing bringing firewood too ah.   220
Then that one the brother said   "Now Sister we will be finished see ah.
We ourselves, will get get done in how will this happen to us?"

He said to her ah.
And the boy doesn't know what to do.
And the girl doesn't know what to do.   225
There is a big pot sitting there.
In it, there is water filling up.
It is filling up with water.
Then one day a dove came and flew in see say ah.
The dove *puuur, tik* (expressive noise).   230

Indeed   the dove looks veeery pretty (said slowly and expressively) it
    seems see say ah.
The pretty dove see has a letter it is said attached to its foot.
A letter is fastened to it.
The dove came and entered he (the boy) took it *mok*.
Then slowly he untied the letter then, it seems that the boy could read
    a little.   235
The boy began to read the letter.
"It is true" it (the letter) says to him ah.

"Now I (the letter) will tell you see ah.

emite, mu, pe kasmarye a.
em pe ti onaynaitti, tukkin na pe, pe tikkar uetki arkwanekala, pe
    na ti onainanaiye a.   240
sappan pe aminait, tukkin na pe, pe okkummakkekala, sappan pe
    aminai takkenye a.
emi peka soko takkenye.
ti kwar, kwar, kwar, kwar nai   mu peka soytakoye.
'pe anka wis totomarkwerye.'
pe muka soko takkenye, 'muye, an pe takkoloye a.   245
iki an totokosun, an wichulitteye a.
pe insa anka totokwerye.'
kep mu peka soytako 'wey pe sao,' mu wepa, totoalir nue totoalir pe
    takker, tup kachikkwa nai takkenye.
tup kachikkwa nait, pe takko, ikkír pe sao, mu arkwatto takkenye a.
mu e purkoye, ittos.   250
peti pe purkosurye.
kep mu purkwisar, kep pe sapan marro soke weki.
espunya nononikko soysunto, espunyar.
e nu ka marroye.
e achu nononikkoye" takken soke.   255
"saliente nuy" soke, "achu saliente.
wese" takken soke, "nu, nu pe marpaloye.
soriente nuypar" takken soke "achu.
pe tek amio takkenye" kar soysunto.
"kep we pe pentakkoeti a   ikar tani takkenye"   kal ikar uylear
    takken soke.   260

napir soke.

pelakwaple kal ikal ikal usku   inso takkarku   tikkar pel onakkwis,
    tii al inso kwakkwarmaali, sus taysisunna a.
peech mu nonite.

mute ipya kwakkwennakwatte soke a.
muu ipya kwakkwenna sokkuti, napir soke.   265
"susmarye anka pe wis totokweloye a.

Now, the grandmother, has caught you ah.
Now you are filling up (the pot) with water, yourselves you, you are
    beside the hot water in order to fall in, you are filling it ah.   240
The firewood you are gathering, for yourselves, in order for you to
    burn it, the firewood you are gathering see ah.
Now I (the letter) will tell you see.
When the water is boiling, boiling, boiling, boiling   the grandmother
    will come and say to you.
'You will dance for me for a while.'
You will say to the grandmother see, 'Grandmother, I will watch you
    first ah.   245
How can I dance, since I do not know how to ah.
You first will dance for me.'
Then the grandmother will come and say to you 'Here is how you do it,'
    that one the grandmother, when you see that she begins to dance
    really begins to dance, there is a rope hanging tightly there see.
And this rope that is hanging tightly there, you will see, *ikkír* you will
    pull it away, so that the grandmother will fall see ah. (The boy will
    use rope to trick/trip grandmother into falling into the boiling water,
    as apparently she had intended to do to him.)
The grandmother she will die, did you hear.   250
And you will not die.
Then when the grandmother has died, then you will cut her belly open
    say here.
A sword will come out say, a sword.
Cut open her breasts.
To get her dog out" see it (the letter) says.   255
"His name is Saliente" it says, "the dog is Saliente.
Here" see it says, "the breast, the breast you will cut open.
And the other's name (other dog who comes out) is Soriente" see it says
    "the dog.
You well will get it (the dog) see" it (the letter) said to him.
"Then he (the dog) will be your helper ah   the way (counsel, in the
    letter) comes see"   the way was given to him see say.   260

It is true it is said.

When the way the way had been all given to them   therefore indeed
    the hot water was all filled up, the water therefore is beginning to
    boil, the boy is sitting seeing this ah.
Finally the grandmother came.

And that one-eyed grandmother it is said ah.
The one-eyed grandmother said it is true it is said.   265
"Children dance for me for a while ah.

tikkar an takket tikkar inso kwa-kwar-may-nai" takken, "nue" soysa
    tayle soke.
kep wepa muu kar soysunna, muu ipya kwakwenna sokkuti, kar soysa,
    "muye   na iki an totokoye?
pan oturtakkwerye."

muu "napir" soke.   270

muu kep totonakuchunto a.
ipya kwakkenna na kwachit tup nai imaysat ki kirrr.
tommo tiyaki
tikkar kwakwarmaynai tikkar kaliente naita a.
oete.   275
muu purkwis.
dead. (Said in English)
(Laughter)
kep mu sulechunto kirr.
kep aki muu kep sapan maricunto weki.
taasssa.   280
espunya nononi, espunya nonos puut.
wesik   nuu marisatki acu nonos saliente.
wesik acu maipali soriente.
macheret appin acu amis takken soke.
napir soysunto a.   285

kepe tayleku   kep punka sokkarsunto "emite napir anmala san
    pentaymala amis takkenye.
nue salayye.
(Pedro drinks.)

Episode III. What happens to the boy and girl at home: Problems with dog/man/husband/ogre

napir soke a.

"emite   anmar tayleku an kamaitimar takken emi teysokku   punye
    weki pe anka   nek etarpekar kuoye.
an   susti   sappurpa naoe   makket."   290
sus makkerpa takuarku a.
teki nanakwichunna.

tata nate nonikkoet, wettar senonikkoet sus.

Hot water I see hot water thus bo-il-ing" see, "good" she said see she
says.
Then that one he (the boy) says to the grandmother, he said to the one-
eyed grandmother, he said to her, "Grandmother now how can I
dance?
You will first teach me."

"Alright" says the grandmother. 270

Then the grandmother was dancing ah.
The one-eyed one tripped on the hanging rope she did *kirrr* (expressive
sound). (Because she could not see she tripped)
Splashing in the water.
The hot water is boiling the hot water is *caliente* (said in Spanish) it is ah.
She passed out. 275
The grandmother died.
Dead (said in English).
(Laughter)
Then the grandmother was pulled out *kirr*.
Then this grandmother is there then her belly was split open.
taasssa (expressive sound). 280
A sword came out, a sword came *puut* (suddenly).
Here from the cut open breast the dog came out *Saliente*.
Here there is another dog *Soriente*.
He got the husband together with his dog (they formed a couple) see say.
It is true it was said ah. 285

Then indeed then he said to his sister "Now it is true we acquired
bodyguards see.
It is good for us."
(Pedro drinks.)

Episode III. What happens to the boy and girl at home: Problems with dog/man/husband/ogre

It is true it is said ah.

"Now we indeed are going about see" now indeed "Sister here you
will stay in order to watch the house for me you will.
I the brother will go to the jungle to hunt." 290
It seems that the brother is quite a hunter ah.
Well he always goes (hunting).

If he would return as the sun disappeared, he would bring back collared
peccary the brother would.

tata nate naoet, wettar senonikkoet.

tek ipakwenkine   acute mai acu suskate acu a.   295
acuka soysa natet.
"ipakwenki tayle an sappur nate (rising pitch).
tule tayleku an yartaynonikkotipaye a.
acu tayleku, iki peka kuar pe takkele (said slowly), ney toypi kual anka
    achu esikkoye a."
punka soysat.   300
punti wismosunnat a.
takkarku   puna   sorpali   maceret se nanakwichi ittos.
pun mm sus sorpa.
macheret achu achu sunna achu se nanakwismosunto.
tek pun yarpar kuti pun yarpar kuti (voice repeatedly diminishes).   305
kep wepa   emi   e punka sokkarsunto "pe suska pe soko takkenye.
'susye tayleku pani tikkasurkus tayleku pane pane pane sappurpa
    nanakus, pane wis puttar ittokus wis pe opunnokoloye.
pe kas nasikko takkenye soke.
wek pe opunnoye.'
kep aki   sus kammai   kep nono pilu appalalakwa   310
    pe   wettar kala yo takken soke a.
sus purkwito, pait wek pe yopaloye.
sus purkoku, pe mette takken temarki pikkin.
tipala.
tipa mettoye.
tipa mettoku   kep na nikkumaloe" achu soytesunto a.   315
napir soke.
punti tayle macheret nukkupimosokku, inso sus istar epinsalearsunto a.
suste e pokwa tanikkit, nue pina pitto saylaki na wilearmalat.
sus pookwat kutiit.
walapala tayle tunkunoniku, sus istar taynonikkit masereunna.   320
aula tayle we ikar saylaki   kirmar aur nappiraki namay takkenye.
we ikar mait.
noar kwen maisuli a.

If he would go as the sun disappeared, he would bring back collared
    peccary.

Well one day   there is a dog it is the boy's dog the dog ah.   *295*
He spoke to the dog as he left.
 (He says to his sister): "One day see if I go to the jungle (rising pitch).
If someone indeed comes to trick me ah.
The dog indeed, if something happens to you you see (said slow), if
    someone wants to enter the house you must let the dog loose for me
    ah."
He said to his sister.   *300*
And the sister knew it also ah.
Indeed   to the sister   afterward (after the brother had left)   there
    comes along a man to her place did you hear.
The sister mm after the brother (had left).
A man a dog a dog in truth a dog (an ogre, dog in form of man) comes
    again and again to her place.
Well the sister lies next to him the sister lies next to him (they make
    love) (voice gradually diminishes).   *305*
Then that one   now   said to the sister "You will tell your brother see.
'Brother indeed you for a long time now indeed are always are going to
    the jungle for me every day every day every day, tomorrow you will
    feel a bit tired you should rest for a little while.
You will hang up a hammock see say.
Here you will rest.'
Then he   while the brother is sleeping   then in the middle of the
    curls of his head (top of the head) you   will stick a collared
    peccary bone see say ah.   *310*
The brother will die, you will stick another one (bone) here.
When the brother has died, you'll throw him see in the sea away.
In the water.
In the water you will throw him.
When you have thrown him in the water   then we will get married"
    the dog said ah.   *315*
It is true it is said.
And the sister see since she also wanted to get married to the man, thus
    she begins to feel hatred for her brother ah.
(Pedro steps out of narrative and says):
The brother the two of them are coming along, listen with care long ago
    these suffering people.
The brother the two of them who were there.
Suddenly see in the middle of growing up, she came to hate her brother
    because of this man.   *320*
Therefore see in earlier times   the uncles (elders) truly used to chant
    about this see.
This story exists.
It is not false ah.

mimmikwa tayleku tunkutaoku na wile taymala   kwenattikwar.
na mas seret nikkupi kualir na kwenatkan istar epinsanmaloe (sounds
    almost unintelligible) anmar?   325
susu   na kwen epinsasuli.
punale   ome nikkuet ular, puna   na pal epinsasurmarye.
we saylaki ma takken soke.
napiri.
teki anmar sokku   inso pun   sus istar epinsalearsunye a.   330
mas seret   pe ikal uysat.
macheret pur napiri ikar nueka ek uysayopi, sus istar epinsalearye.
kep sus kammai   kep sus tayleku pun imachun takkenye.
emi nono pilu appalalakwa, tayleku   wettar kar yos takkenye.
kep pina appalalakwa   emi   emi wettar nukar yos pali.   335
purkwis sus.
kep tipa mette PIKKÍN.
achute pule kuarye, achu e achu.
aaa e achu pe takke nek unkepi kualit a.
wepa pun kek takkarmoku esiysasunto.   340
mm achu appaRRmai.
sus purkwenait kep katap ti yaki a.
il ili akkwampa yok se nonisunto.
acu elo elo elo elo elo elo elo elo (gets softer) napa ar uun imaysa.
weki ar un imaysa, achu elonasunto, el el.   345
sus turkuarto a.
sus turkus.
sus turkusku sokkarsunto, "weti ipikarye a?"
napir soke.
"pun tek tek tek an imaysa."   350
napir.

kep   sus pinsaarmosunna   "emi tayleku   ipi unale pun istar an
    epinsaartipaye a?
ikar aminakwarsunto."
takkarku, macheretse nanakwichi.
kep achuka sokkarsunna "emi   ipi tule   nanakwistipeye an
    punseyye?   355

Children indeed while they grow up love one another   within the
    family.
If they want to get married why must they feel hatred for their own
    family members why do we?   325
She didn't think of him   as a brother.
And this sister   because of getting married, the sister   disliked him
    (her brother).
This is what in earlier times used to happen see say.
It is true.
Well we said   thus the sister   begins to feel hatred for her brother
    ah.   330
The husband   gave you (= her) the way (counsel).
As if her husband gave her a truer way a better one, she began to feel
    hatred for her brother.
Then while her brother is lying sleeping   then to her brother indeed his
    sister did it see.
Now in the middle of his head's curl (top of head), indeed   she stuck
    the collared peccary bone see.
Then in the middle of his chest   now   she stuck also the collared
    peccary tooth.   335
He died the brother did.
Then she threw him in the water away *PIKKÍN.*
And his dog got very angry, the dog his dog.
Aah his dog you see he wanted to get away (from the pole to which
    he is attached) ah.
That one the sister is also astonished that he (the dog) got away.   340
Mm the dog is ruNNing.
While the brother is dying then he (the dog) grabbed him in the water ah.
He pulled and pulled suddenly he came up the bank.
The dog licks licks licks licks licks licks licks licks (gets softer) he did
    only that.
He did only that, the dog was licking him, licking licking.   345
The brother came back to life ah.
The brother was brought back to life.
When the brother came back to life he said, "Why did this happen ah?"
It is true it is said.
"Sister well well well did it to me."   350
It is true.

Then   the brother thought also   "Now indeed   for what reason did
    my sister begin to feel hatred for me ah?
I will first go and get this way (figure this out)."
Indeed, he goes to the husband's place.
Then he said to his dog   "Now   who is the person   who could
    be going to my sister's place?   355

teysokku ikar yalaki   anmar meko" takken soysunto a.

nanananamait ittos.

achu   PALIMAKKOETIT acute an pey soket.

soeti.

achute   e nue parnae.   360

ipikan anmar achu   pe   pe ittos sursi a?

pepa impakwenale   pe ipetile   nuekampi   achu   ikar   mai
    napir tak sursi.

teki aunale, we ikar masunto.

teysokku teki kusku   kepe   achu taylearku   ikar yarki mekwichunto
    a.

susti nipa mekwismoka.   365

toytar   wilupparta tule ootake.

nia machi selet tani soysunto a.

o-ta-ker-pi-ni

kep i-may-no-ni-ku   ikarki kwichi kep, maynonisunnat a.

maynonisunna, nia purkoto a.   370

nia purkoku, pun ulutamokoet.

kep sus ka soytisunto a.

"anmar wese ukaymarsunye a.

pe istar an tak an pe   parwiculi ittos."

Episode IV. The boy's final adventure: The boy saves a village from an ogre

sus wakkittesunto nakaate.   375

achute nisatte ittos.

kepe tayleku natap natap natap natap (gets softer) immmakke neka
    paitse sus toytapkua.

kep tule wilepukkwat neyse toytap takken soke a.

tule takkarku   wileket nappa aaii   neka tar tummakan tayleku pela
    yaakana per sulemai, mimmi pippikwa sulemai, "toa an pentakko"
    soysunto a?

kirmar wilepukkwat.   380

saylaki nek tanikki.

machikwate   pinsatanisunnat etto.

weki pe nekkunanae etto.

pe takko takken soke a.

"unni an pe pentakkotipaye," machikwa sokkar takken soke.   385

napir.

takker kepye.

Therefore we will lie down   beside the path" see he said ah.

Many (people) go by did you hear.

 (Pedro explains):

The dog   WILL BE A PURSUER this dog will I tell you.

He is a hunter.

And the dog   he chases well.   360

 (Pedro speaks out of story):

Why do we (talk) about the dog   you   did you hear ah.

Perhaps if you are the owner   good   of a dog   the dog's   way is
     there   he likes you.

Well for this reason, the story was there.

Therefore well it happened   then   the dog it seems   lay down beside
     the path ah.

And the brother he is also lying up above (in a tree).   365

After   some time went by a person shooows up.

It is the ogre-husband who is coming it is said ah.

He-is-ac-tu-al-ly-show-ing-up.

Then he came-and-did-it   he (the ogre) is standing in the path then, (the
     brother) came and killed him ah.

He came and killed him, the ogre will die ah.   370

When the ogre has died, the sister will also get angry.

Then her brother said to her ah.

"This is it as far as we're concerned ah.

Since you hate me I don't   know you anymore did you hear."

Episode IV. The boy's final adventure: The boy saves a village from an ogre

The boy abandoned the place and he went away.   375

And the dog he took him did you hear.

Then indeed he went along he went along he went along he went along
     (gets softer) he diiid until the brother got to and entered another place.

Then he got to and and entered a place of many suffering people see say
     ah.

The people so   are suffering what a suffering land aaii   a big place
     indeed all the young girls are taken away, the small children are taken
     away, "Who will help us?" they said ah.

The uncles (elders) are all suffering.   380

In earlier times things were like this.

And the boy   this is what he came along thinking about.

This you (see) is how things were.

You will see see say ah.

"If only I would be able to help you," the boy said see say.   385

It is true.

"Let's see then."

kepe tayleku machikwa aki tayleku kep kirmar pentaysokkar takken
    soke.
kirmar taylearku pela inso taylekua   tule per
(woman says "shit;" not about story)
per tayle kirkumai.
tule warkwen tise nao per yokkumai.   390
takkarku   emi nia tummat, nekurpa mait.
a kwaple tule kamai takken soke a.
tule walikkuetsuli.
kep a tayle e rey tayleku pinsamasunto, "toa an pentakkoye?
tule an pentaysar kep an siskwa, nuet tiit, kal an ukkoye a.   395
an siskwa takkenye."
kep machikwa soytesunna, "ani an pe pentakkoye.
takker kepye a."

kep aki tayleku machikwate kin arpaarsunto takken soke.
takkarku nia pait kuti moka.   400
kep soktesunto omekwakala.
"olo arkan, an peka ukkoye a.
yoetse   tule soytakoe, 'ani an pe pentasye.'
kep an olo arkan yoitki an takko takkenye, aa pankat olo arkan kannar
    panka ukkoye.
yo tule an yartakkoet an wisye, ittos."   405
olo arkan kal uysa takken soke.
ome olo arkan yochunna   arpaarsunto.
tek nai nai nai (gets softer) takkarku inso   machikwate taylearku, inso
    pela inso kirmar pentayna kuarsunto.
"espunya yosatki, an nek appalala yochunto SWATA."
wepa immar tummat nakkwialile, kwiskunonitae, nek appalala a.   410
purkwenonisunto ittos, nia tummatti, purkwis.
a purkwisku, soylearsunna, "toa we an an pentasye a?"
nia kottesunto.
"ani takkenye."
"suli pe suli ar   machikwate ampa   ampa yokkumai a.   415
e pentaysat."
aunal ipakwenkine   tule immar napir immaysat   we anmar sok "ani
    an kusye."
suli pe kuchuli a.
tule kusat yokkutta takkenye.

Then indeed the boy in this place indeed then he is about to help the
     uncles see say.
The elders indeed are all thus indeed   all the people
(woman says "shit," not about story)
they are all see perishing.
If a person goes to the river he disappears completely.   390
So   now there is a big ogre, below the earth he is.
He is grabbing all the people see say ah.
People cannot approach him.
Then he see the king (of these poor people) indeed was thinking, "Who
     will help us?
The person who helps us then my daughter, who is pretty, I will give
     her to him ah.   395
My daughter see."
Then the boy said, "Me I will help you.
Let's see then ah."

Then in this indeed the boy began to work for this see say.
So there is another ogre also.   400
Then he (the boy) said to his wife (to be).
"I will give you, a gold ring (marriage ring) ah.
One day   some (other) person will come to say, 'Me I helped you.'
Then my gold ring that you are wearing I see see, aah you will have to
     give me my gold ring back. (When I've done my job)
Later if someone tricks me I would know, did you hear."   405
He gave the gold ring to her see say.
His wife put the gold ring on   and he began to work.
Well working working working (gets softer) so thus   and the boy it
     seems, thus completely thus was beginning to help the uncles.
"A sword I placed, I placed it in the middle of his body (of the ogre)
     SWATA."
That one that big guy when he got up, it was standing, in the middle
     of his body ah.   410
He died did you hear, the big ogre, he died.
When he died, it was said, "Who helped us ah?"
A (another) ogre called out.
"It was me see."
(People say):
"No it was not you   and the boy he was still   was still gone ah. 415
He was the one who helped."
(Pedro speaks, gives moral):
For this reason if one day   a person did something well   a (another)
     person says to us "I'm the one who did it."
No it was not you ah.
The person who did it always gets denied (never gets credit) see.

aula saylay tule immar immaymalatti, ikarka kuchurtae, sorpa "immar
    immaysat IKKÍR."   420
sulettae sanakkwa.
auna anmar tey kwen nappa nek na kusye, we ikarki mai par takken
    soke a.
we ikala   nappira mai takken soke a.
kwen noarsurye.
teysokku wekimalat ikarkinti, pe nue, ittoalile   nappirakwa
    papkan   saylaki we ikar mait.   425
tule soke "kwentoye."
kwento suli.
nappira mai a.
istoria maiyop ittolesunto takken soke a.
anmarkat, tulekatse istoria nue mamoye.   430
anmartina   ikar teysik nuekwa amisurtasokku.
pinsa ikar suliye anmar pititi takkenye.
nue ittoer ikar nue mamoye.
weti wese peka sokkarsunto pittokua.
suitti maina tese.   435

Joel Sherzer asks: suitti?
Pedro responds:
eye ikar suitti.
walapala pe soysa.

Therefore in earlier times the people who do things, never get credit for
    the way (achievement), afterward (another person says) "I did the
    thing *IKKÍR*."   420
The same ones (the bad ones) are chosen.
For this reason we well in this world were like this, this way (of
    behaving) is there again see say ah.
This way   is truly there see say ah.
It is not false.
Therefore these ways, if you learn, them well   it is true they belong to
    the fathers   in earlier times these ways were there.   425
People say "It is a story."
It's not a story.
It's the truth ah.
It is like history it seems see say ah.
It is ours, the Kuna people's history and it is a good one also.   430
And we   if we don't acquire (study) such good ways.
For the fun of it we claim we do not have ways see.
There are many good ways good for listening.
Up to here I tell you you have heard.
It is long to the end.   435

Joel Sherzer asks: Long?
Pedro responds:
Yes it is a long way.
I told you a part of it.

Figure 5. *King of village presents his daughter to boy*

Chapter 3

The One-Eyed Grandmother

Written and read by Hortenciano Martínez

This version of *The One-Eyed Grandmother* was written and then read orally by Hortenciano Martínez on July 8, 1970. While many Kuna read and write Spanish, it is only recently that they have been writing in the Kuna language. Hortenciano Martínez, my assistant at the time, had listened to and transcribed Pedro Arias's telling (chap. 2) and spontaneously added a different version to the notebook in which he had made the transcription, a version that he had heard. After writing it down, he read it aloud and I taped his reading.

Hortenciano Martínez's version of *The One-Eyed Grandmother* shares certain features with Pedro Arias's, but is quite different. The grandmother plays a much smaller, in fact tiny, role, even though she still gives the story its name. The focus is on a family in which a sister is married to an ogre who kills off his brothers-in-law, until one of them, through miraculous feats and trickery, in particular using an eyelash to replace a tree limb, defeats the ogre.

As in Pedro Arias's version of the story, the boy comes upon a village and, after killing a monster, a seven-headed dog, marries its leader's daughter. But at the end of this version, the boy is suddenly killed by his own sister, angry at him for having killed her ogre/husband. The black man who appears at the end of the story reflects the ambiguous and ambivalent relations between Kunas and blacks. The Kuna come into frequent contact with both Colombian and Panamanian blacks. While the Kuna are friendly toward blacks, and interact with them in their typical playful way, they also express negative attitudes toward blacks. They are especially concerned about Kuna women having relations with blacks. This version of the story, like Pedro Arias's, also reflects the tensions among family loyalties, deceptions, and betrayals. There is much more violence in this story than there is in ordinary Kuna life, perhaps due to its European sources, perhaps to its Latin American indigenous mythical relations.

Because it was written before it was told, this version of *The One-Eyed Grandmother* is special and unique with regard to the other texts in this book. Hortenciano Martínez was a young man in his early twenties at the time. He had lived and studied in Spanish in Panama City and had never seen Kuna stories in written form. At the same time, he respected and appreciated his culture and was particularly fascinated by its verbal practices. He drew on these in his reading/telling of the story, including the direct quotation of characters and the use of onomatopoetic words.

In Olokwagdi de Akwanusadup's illustration for this story (fig. 6), the boy directs his dog to attack the ogre, and the dog does so by biting him in the testicles. The ogre is both monstrous and humanlike. He carries an axe, as Kuna men often do when working in the jungle. Both the ogre and the boy are dressed as Olokwagdi imagines the Kuna to have dressed traditionally. A Kuna house can be seen in the distance in this jungle scene.

My photograph (photo 2) shows Hortenciano Martínez writing in a notebook.

Here is the story.

Figure 6. Boy directs dog to attack ogre

Kuna

ipakwenki, taylear soke.
masmala warpaa.
we masmala pun niy soysunto.
e pun nia nikkuma soke.
ipakwenki   ia sokkarsunto.   5
"wis nakoloye."
aki mu ipya kwakkwenna   si takkarsunto.
mu taylearkua   machise mas ekicharunto, machi ka sokkuti.
"wis unnilasar an"   taynatammoye.
taylearku, upmar muttik   purkwema purkwema tato.   10
ia tummat   purkwisa   teki sokkuti, ia yarpalit.
"namokweloye."
mu appinkwarparto.
teka   tekka mu sokkarparto   machikwa.
tey soytemoto a   e ia   soysatki.   15
teki ia yarpalit, purkwitmoto.
takkarku   up upmar   opurkemait.
urpa   soymokuti   "namokweloye."
takkarmoku, mu apinkuarmoto.
mu sokkuti, machikwaka.   20
"wis mas an   apemoye."
"tekka" sokkuti machi.
"tek, anmar itu ikar, pap mesis sokkuti.
wis peka   ukkerkemmoye."
teki ka   mu sokkarsunto   "pe pun pey   soytaoye.   25
'pe kalu nakapa pe mekoye'   pey soytapaloye.
'pe achu   aila urpa pe   mesoye.
pe kannir   aila urpa   pe   sioye'   pey soytepaloye.
'siku   aila urpa pe, sapokoye.'
ka pe   sokeye   'immar kwaple an kas urpa   anpakuetpiye.   30
kusku pap anmar itu ikar mesisnatmoye.'
ar pinsa   pe yartaynaitteye."
teki machikwa, neyse nonisunto.
pun kwaple immar sokkarsunto   mu ka soysat.
machikwa   punka sokkarsunto a.   35
"immar kwaple   an kas, urpa, kapetpiye."
teki   muttik kusku   up es epillear ittole, teki   muttik kusku   up
    machikwase   ar ittolesunto.
appin wepa   achu uruar ittole teki   upte e kas maitse, aparmaisi
    ittole.
tek nek oipochunto.

English

One day, see say.
There are three boys.
And these three boys have a sister it is said.
Their sister is married to an ogre it is said.
One day   the older brother said.   5
"I am going away for a while (to the jungle)."
There he met   a one-eyed grandmother who is there.
The grandmother indeed   asked the boy for food ah, the boy said to
    her.
"I do not have much"   they went to see.
Indeed, the brothers-in-law at night   are dying are dying always.   10
The older brother   died   well he said, the next oldest brother did.
"I will go too."
He too met the grandmother.
Well   well the grandmother again said (asked for food)   the boy
    (said no).
Well he said ah   what his older brother   said.   15
Well the next oldest brother, died too.
So   the brother-in-law is killing the brothers-in-law.
The younger brother   says also   "I will go too."
So also, he also met the grandmother.
The grandmother said, to the boy.   20
"I want a little   food."
"Well" said the boy.
"Well, because Father (God) left, a road before us it is said.
I must give you   a little."
Well the grandmother   said to him   "Your sister will say   to you. 25
'You must lie down beside the wall'   she will say to you again.
'Your dog   you must put below   the storage shelf.
Your chicken   below the storage shelf   you   must put'   she will
    say to you.
'Your arrow   below the storage shelf you, must store.'
You say   to her   'All things are under   my hammock.   30
Because that is how Father before us left the way.'
Because she is tricking you   for the fun of it."
Well the boy, came home.
His sister told him all the things   the grandmother had said to him.
The boy   said to his sister ah.   35
"The things are all   below, my hammock, for sleeping only."
Well   at night   his brother-in-law began to sharpen his machete,
    well   at night   the brother-in-law approached   the boy he did.
But that one   the dog began to bark he did well   and the brother-in-
    law went to his hammock, running he does.
Well dawn came.

tek ney muttikkuspali   kapikwenkusku   ittole wepa upte es
   epillearpa ittole.   40
tek machi, maitse   arparsunto.
up walikusku, achute, uluarparsunto.
teki upte, aparmaisiparsunto.
e kache.
yamu upte   kamaiyop, imachunto a.   45
asa NOOOOR.
tek nek oipposparsunto.
upte machika, sokkuti, "anmar pan sappurpa, namaloye."
teki natmarsunto sappi tummat walikusku.
up machika sokkuti   "sappi nipa pe, nakkwekwerye.   50
pe takko takkenye.
pule nek tikkasurkus anmar opetaniye."
teki up   nakkwichunto, nipa kusku.
nipa kusku upte, sokkuti ka, "anse pe, perye" teki niate sappi,
   sikkarsunto.
wepa sappi taylekusku sirikkwakus   soysunto.   55
teki machi pinsarkua "iki saoe?"
teki kep   ipya sika kakwen   unnutsunto.
piKKIN soye.
wepa sappi kanarsi yop mai.
machite par pulosta   urwet.   60
kannar sateparto.
sappi sikket   wepa kannar   sappi sirikkwakus tayleta.
machi pinsarparsunto.
"iki sapaloe?"
ipya sika aparkinet   kakwen   unnuspar tayleta.   65
piKKIN soye.
kannar sappi kannar yop kwichi   niate palitar pulosta.
urwet.
kannar nia sappi, sikket nasitpartole.
taylearku sappi   kannar sirikkwakusku, wepa taylearku, achute,
   winnaet, kekkus, naimota.   70
ar machikwate   punka soysa alit, "wepa achu   winnapi kualir pe
   takker   pe echikkoye.
tekir pe, echiysulir, nek malutoye."
teysokku punte achu   echis ittolesunto.
wepa takkarku.
achute.   75
kwapunnumakketani tayleta.
machite ka sokkuti   "caliente colienteye.
isturkeye."
wep achute   aluki kas, taylemota.

Well it became night again   and at midnight   that one the brother-
in-law began to sharpen his machete again.   40
Well he went, to where   the boy was.
And beside the brother-in-law, the dog, began to bark again.
Well and the brother-in-law, he goes running again.
To his hammock.
And the brother-in-law (the boy) pretends   that he is sleeping, he did
like that ah.   45
Asa NOOOOR.
Well dawn came again.
And the brother-in-law, said to the boy, "We will go tomorrow, to the
jungle."
Well they went beside a big tree.
The brother-in-law said to the boy   "You will climb up, the tree.   50
You will see see.
How far we have left to come here."
Well the brother-in-law   climbed up, to the very top.
And when he was on the very top the brother-in-law, said to him, "By me
you will be finished well" and the ogre began to cut, the tree.
When this tree indeed was sliced to a point (about to fall)   it is said. 55
Well the boy thought "What can be done?"
Well then   he pulled out   one eyelash.
He threw it AWAY it is said.
And that tree gets like it was before.
And that guy got furious   he was angry.   60
He did it again.
He cut the tree   and again   the tree was sliced to a point see.
The boy thought.
"What can be done again?"
Again he pulled out   one   eyelash in the middle see.   65
He threw it AWAY it is said.
Again the tree again stands as before   and the ogre again was furious.
He was angry.
Again the ogre cut, the tree.
Indeed the tree   again was sliced to a point, that one indeed, the dog,
there, wanted to pee, but couldn't.   70
For the boy   had said to his sister as he left, "If the dog   wants to
pee you see   you will let him go.
Well if you, don't let him go, the house will cave in."
Therefore the sister let   the dog go hear.
And that one (the dog) so.
The dog.   75
He came with his tail moving see.
And the boy said to them (there were two dogs)   "Caliente Colienteye.
Attack."
And that one the dog   grabbed him by the balls, see.

up purkwit. 80
machi natparsunto.
wepa   taynatapku, ome   ti aparki   kannaresi.
pakkakwar   tayle soysunto.
machite ka soysunto   "ipu pe sasie?"   omete ka, soysunna   "an tule
    wile takkarku, achu nono   kwakuylet   kachi" soysunto.
ka machite soysunna, "an pe pentakkoye." 85
ka ome soysunna, "tule ichesulir pela, an pentachulirye.
pe pursun takkenye.
peti unni walakwenatteye."
machi ka sokkuti, "pe an takkoenye" soysunto.
wepa achu ka soysunto. 90
caliente coliente isturye.
teki achu tummatte, purkwichunto.
teki ome   e papte, ipa onoarsunto.
taylearku, chichit   kannaresi aparki.
ome yalapa si tayleta. 95
sichitte.
ar ome papte soysata, "tule sichitir, sippukwatir, an siskwa   nikkuo
    takkenye.
pentaysar   takkenye."
wepa machite   takkwichunto   NUUUU.
"sichit an yartaysa"   e achuka, sokkarsunto. 100
"pe patte sunao takkenye."
tummatipeye.
achu natsunto   patte ikkir soye.
tummate sokkuti.
e policiamarka "we   achupa pe na takkenye. 105
toa e ipettipaye?"
policiate achupa   arsunto, takkarku   ka sokkuti, "we achu pe kat?"
    sokeye.
"eye" ka soysunna.
"we achu   an kat takkenye."
machi sokkuti, "tummat anka kornaye 'we machi.'" 110
tummat tek arsunto.
ka sokkuti, "ipika pe anse korkwisye?"
machite ka soysunto.
"an pe siskwa pentaysatteye."
ka tummat sokkuti, "pinsa pe an yartakkwisye. 115

The brother-in-law died.   80
The boy took off again.
While   he was going along he saw, a woman   sitting there   in the
    middle of a river.
Good looking   see it is said.
And the boy said to her   "What are you sitting doing?"   and the
    woman says, to him   "I am a miserable person so, I am trapped
    by a dog   with seven heads" she said.
And the boy says to her, "I will help you."   85
The woman says to him, "No matter how many people there are, they
    could not help me.
You are one see.
Since you are all by yourself."
The boy said to her, "You will see me" he said.
To that one the dog he said to him.   90
Caliente, Coliente attack.
Well and the big animal, he died.
Well the woman   her father, was beginning to have a big festival.
Indeed, a black guy   is sitting there in the middle.
He is sitting next to the woman see.   95
The black guy.
Now the woman's father said, "If a person is black, or if he is white,
    he will marry   my daughter see.
If he would help (free her)   see."
And that one the boy   was standing looking   NUUUU.
"The black guy tricked me"   he said, to his dog.   100
"You will take away his plate see."
The big one's (the chief's).
The dog left   he took the plate away it is said.
And the big one (the chief) said.
To his police (guards) "You   go with that dog see.   105
(To see) who is his owner?"
And the police went with   the dog, so   they said to him, "Is this
    dog yours?" they say.
"Yes" he says to them.
"This dog   is mine see."
The boy says, "Go call the big one (the chief) for me 'hey boy.'"   110
The chief well he came.
He (the chief) says to him (the boy), "Why did you call me?"
The boy said to him.
"Because I helped your daughter."
The big one said to him, "You are standing here tricking me for the
    fun of it.   115

ar sichit anka   e non senonikkitte."
machi ka soysunna   "pe an takkoye," wepa machite, ol arkan, onoar
    tayteta.
tummat sokkuti, "we sichit   an yartaiti" tayleye, e sortakanka sokkuti,
"sichit   opurkwemarye.
an yartaytiye."
teki sichit opurkwelearsunto.   120
teki machit   ome yalapa   sikwis taylesunta.
teki machi ome nikkus   kannar pun taytappali   pun nukkupirki,
    meinoni soysunto.
punte napir ittotisulitte   e machere opurkwisatpa.
teki punte   nono pilu appallalla   ikko, yotsunto.
machi purkwis.   125
ase kwento   maisunto.
mu ipya kwakkwenna.

For the black guy brought   me his head" (proof that he had saved the
   daughter).
The boy says to him   "You will see," and he the boy, took out, a
   wedding ring see.
The big one said, "It was the black guy   who was tricking me" see, he
   said to his followers, "kill   the black guy."
The one who was tricking me.
Well they killed the black guy.   120
Well the boy   sat down   next to the woman see.
Well the boy married the woman   he went to see his sister again   he
   came to sit, on her lap it is said.
And since his sister was really angry   for he had killed her husband.
Well the sister   stuck a needle   in the middle, of the curls of his head.
The boy died.   125
That is the end   of the story.
The One-Eyed Grandmother.

Figure 7. Jaguar and Turtle exhausted after race

Chapter 4

The Turtle Story

Told by Chief Nipakkinya

Chief Nipakkinya of Mulatuppu told *yalamoro kwento/ The Turtle Story* in April 1970. Nipakkinya was at the time an elderly chief who was re- spected for his knowledge and performing abilities and also was loved for his exuberant and friendly sense of humor. He was known and loved throughout Kuna Yala for his humorous exploits and storytelling abili- ties. The story was told to me and my assistant Hortenciano Martínez in my house.

Nipakkinya told *The Turtle Story* to me as his addressee/responder (he calls me "my friend" in the narration, which is a quite common way of addressing a responder during storytelling) with Hortenciano Martínez as the audience. He modulates his voice with regard to tempo, volume, and pitch to animate the narration, especially the voices of the two ani- mal actors, Turtle and Jaguar.

The Turtle Story, like other Kuna animal stories and many animal sto- ries all over Native America and indeed the world, has two protagonists, with different physical characteristics and personality traits, who oppose and trick one other. The protagonists in this story are Turtle, who gives the story its name, and Jaguar. Jaguar is powerful, wily, and feared, but also clumsy, the Kuna version of the Central and South American jag- uar, of both natural and mythological significance throughout the region. He always wants to eat his opponents, in this case Turtle. Turtle is clever and wins out through trickery.

Jaguar challenges Turtle to a race or competition and says that if he wins he will eat Turtle. Turtle accepts and off they go. The story consists of two episodes. In the first episode, widespread in the Americas and all over the world, Turtle calls on other turtles to line up from the starting line to the finish line and therefore give the impression of having won.[1]

The second, scatological episode is a defecation contest to see who eats more animals, as evidenced by the animal skins one eliminates.[2] Turtle comically survives this contest as well. The two episodes have parallel codas (lines 30–32 and 77–82), focusing on the fact that the two animals will not eat one another and that they have become/will remain good friends.

Central to this story is the Kuna word *yalatakke. Yalatakke* has several overlapping and combined meanings in Kuna, "race," "compete," and "trick." They are all involved in this story and are salient according to the context in which *yalatakke* occurs. I have dealt with this in the translation by using both "race" and "compete," allowing "trick" to emerge as an underlying, implicit motif. The story has no overt moral, message, or explanatory element. It does have an implicit message, or set of implicit messages.

The humor of this story is a result of the combination of its referential contents, its linguistic details, and Nipakkinya's telling. With regard to referential contents, Turtle's statement, line 79, that "we will not eat each other" is particularly funny, in that it is Jaguar who is intending to eat Turtle and not the other way around, which, in any case, would be quite a feat. More generally, the fact that the two animals speak to one another in colloquial Kuna and interact in very Kuna ways is an important feature of the story's overall humorous tone.

A good example of a linguistic detail used humorously involves the positional suffixes of verbs. These suffixes are an optional grammatical category, which depict four body positions the subject of a Kuna verb can be in—standing, sitting, lying, or perched.[3] Since they are optional, their use is marked, bringing out the salience and often humor of a particular activity. When the turtles call out in the race, they are described as *kolemai* "calling in a lying position," emphasizing the fact that turtles are flat, horizontal on the ground. This is how Turtle deploys many turtles to trick Jaguar.

In the second episode, Jaguar defecates, humanlike, sitting with his eyes closed. Turtle imitates him, moving from his usual lying position to a very funny sitting position, also with his eyes closed. It is because Jaguar has his eyes closed that Turtle is able to trick him by stealing his excrement.

While this story has links to animal stories throughout Native America and the world more generally, it is transformed and shaped into a Kuna telling. Thus, while in some versions Turtle wins and his opponent dies, in the Kuna version, no one wins (they are tied), no one dies, and the two protagonists end up friends, no doubt to compete and trick each other again at a later date. In addition, this Kuna telling combines two distinct stories into two episodes of a single and related one.[4]

Kuna ecology, beliefs, and practices are important in this story. Eating is a daily preoccupation and source of anxiety as well as humor. Eating of meat involves prestige as well as nourishment. It is the sign of a good hunter who has resources to share with others. The Kuna love to hunt and to talk about hunting. At the same time, the quantity of game is rapidly dwindling in the Kuna environment, and it is more and more rare that Kuna eat freshly killed animals.

The constant bantering between the two protagonists is a playful rendering of Kuna everyday verbal interactions. Nipakkinya intersperses his own commentary into these short, rapidly uttered, humorous conversational interchanges.

Although an informal telling of a humorous story, Nipakkinya's structuring of *The Turtle Story* has affinities and continuities with Kuna discourse more generally, including formal and ritual discourse. There is considerable grammatical and semantic parallelism, the hallmark of Kuna ritual speech. An excellent example is provided by lines 33–43 in episode 2. The following conversational frame is repeated three times, for three animals in the Kuna jungle environment that are considered good for eating—collared peccary, agouti, and deer—turning it into a stylized question and answer routine:

> Jaguar: "Animal X in truth do you eat?"
> Turtle: "Animal X in truth I eat/do" Turtle says.
> "I in truth eat it also" he says.

The Turtle Story is both a model of and a model for Kuna social and cultural life and Kuna verbal performance. According to Kuna belief, animals were once people. Because of their bad behavior, including especially their trickster behavior, they became animals. But they still retain some of their human characteristics. They behave like humans in many ways, including conversational joking and tricking. So while ostensibly a story about two animals in the Kuna ecology, this is also a story about Kuna humans, including such daily Kuna emotions and concerns as hunger, pain, and death, and competition, rivalry, and antagonism between individuals in the same community. But at the same time this story is also a fictional account of real animals, which the Kuna observe every day and appreciate as part of the unique natural world that is theirs and is most significant to them.

The Turtle Story is thus a model of what animals are like and what humans are sometimes like but should not be. It is also a model for appropriate human behavior—one should not threaten/fight with/kill/eat others, but should rather play and joke and go on with life.

Nipakkinya's way of telling and structuring *The Turtle Story* is also a model of and model for Kuna speaking practices more generally. The use of grammatical and semantic parallelism, the quoting and enactment of the various characters, and the expressive use of the voice more generally all reflect the Kuna ideal of verbal performance. They are also a model for the way these same devices are more formally elaborated in ritual genres of speaking and chanting.

Olokwagdi de Akwanusadup's illustrations are imaginative and humorous, just like Nipakkinya's telling of the story that inspired them. Jaguar and Turtle are both very animal and very human. They cry big tears, are physically as well as emotionally exhausted, smile, and shake hands. We see them in a very dense jungle, full of plants, trees, and water. In figure 7, Turtle, very humanlike, is standing up. In both illustrations, Jaguar wears the cloth skirt that Olokwagdi imagines men to have worn in earlier times. The friendly handshake at the end of the story and in figure 8 shows that among animals, as among humans, friendship, understanding, and collaboration are the best practice. My photograph (photo 3) is of the teller, Chief Nipakkinya, sitting with other village leaders, watching a youth sporting event.

Here is the story.[5]

Figure 8. Jaguar and Turtle shake hands

Kuna

Episode I

soke a.

achu   yalamoro   e pokwa   yalatakke soke a.
aha.
yalamoro   e   sikwe.
kwatulakwena.
kakkattar sikwisa.   5
ile sikwe.
achu epo "yalatakke" soke (said fast).
teki "yalatakke" soke.
aha nueti.
na tare nanae.   10
a.
yalatakkoe a aparmakke.
tare.
a.
pitti pule nanae?
"pe akkue nanaele   pe anse kulleko ittosa.
pe, an yopi nanaele.   15
an pe kunnosuli a.
melle an pe kunnoe.
pe akku nanaele, an pe kunno."
aha   napirto.
teysokku yalatakke   etto nuet.   20
teki yalatakkena.
kole.
a emiski nae apparmakte a (higher pitch with more voice modulation).
m.
nate nate, kolemai.
"anna," kwen kole, "oi" kwen "oi." (quoted portions in higher pitch). 25
"an we mosa, an we mosa," kolemai a (quoted portions in higher pitch
    with more voice modulation).
untar   "mosa" kwen "mosa."
aa na a tare a.
aha yerpa.
key na akkalomala.   30
"melle an pe par kunsunno ittos" mm.
"ukakka, ai nueti" soke.

English

Episode I

It is said ah.

Jaguar   Turtle   the two of them   they are racing ah.
Aha
Turtle   he   takes his place.
Twenty of them.
Twenty-five of them took their places.   5
They place themselves in line.
Jaguar the two of them "race" they say (said fast).
Well "race" they say.
Aha good.
Equally they go along.   10
Ah.
They are going to race ah they are running.
Equal.
Ah.
Which one goes along faster?
"If you do not go   you will be eaten by me did you hear.
If you, go the same as me.   15
I will not eat you ah.
No I won't eat you.
If you do not go, I will eat you."
Aha   it is true.
So they race   alright good.   20
Well they are going to race.
They call out.
Ah now off they go they begin to run ah (higher pitch with more voice
    modulation).
m.
They are off they are off, they are lying calling.
"Hey," one calls "hey," another one "hey" (quoted portions in higher
    pitch).   25
"I got there, I got there," they are lying calling ah (quoted portions in
    higher pitch with more voice modulation).
And   "I got there" another one "I got there."
Aah indeed ah tied ah.
Aha good.
They could do no more.   30
"No I will not be able to eat you did you hear" mm.
"That is it for now, good friend" it is said.

Episode II

"pe   sunna pe   immar kunne (in this and succeeding lines, quoted
  portions are generally louder)?
wetarra sunna pe kunne?"
aha.
"weterra sunna   an" yalamoro soke.   35
"an   sunna kunnemoka" soke.
"an kunne napiri kunne wetarra ittos."
mm.
"usu sunna pe kunne?"
"usu sunna an kunne."
aha.
"an sunna kunnemoka."   40
aha.
"koe sunna pe kunne?"
"koe sunna an kunnemoka.
an sunna kunnemoka" aha.
yerpa.
pela immar.   45
etto, takkemala.
yalatakke.
satue a.
"pe apsar pule apsa walakwena.
pe sa.   50
pe apsar walakwena.
napir.
na taremaloe.
kwenti anka pe kakkansaele.
akku an pe ittoke.   55
melle kakkansae nappirrakwa."
aha.
achu e insa satukolo.
"an insa satukolo ittosa."
achu satusa ipya murru.
ipya murru satue.   60
yalamoro   takkesi weki si moka.
yalamoro sue a.
e sa.
onirisa e katseka.

aha.
atto.   65
takke.
"sa an takke (this line spoken very softly).

Episode II

"Do you   in truth do you   eat animals (in this and succeeding lines,
    quoted portions are generally louder)?
Collared peccary in truth do you eat?"
Aha.
"Collared peccary in truth   I do"   Turtle says.   35
"I   in truth eat it also" he says.
"I eat in truth I eat collared peccary did you hear."
Mm.
"Agouti in truth do you eat?"
"Agouti in truth I eat."
Aha.
"I in truth eat it also."   40
Aha.
"Deer in truth do you eat?"
"Deer in truth I eat also.
I in truth eat it also" aha.
Good.
All animals.   45
So indeed, let us see.
Let us race (compete).
At shitting ah.
(Jaguar says) "(If) your (animal) skins more (animal) skins alone.
Your shit.   50
Your (animal) skins alone.
It is true (are the same as mine).
Once again we will be tied.
Now if you lie to me.
I would not like you.   55
Do not lie reeeally."
Aha.
Jaguar he will shit first.
"I will shit first did you hear."
Jaguar shat with his eye clooosed
With his eyes clooosed he shits.   ·60
Turtle   is sitting seeing this he sits down also.
Turtle gathers ah.
His (Jaguar's) shit.
He moved it over to his own place.

Aha.
So indeed.   65
Look.
(Jaguar says) "It *is* shit I *see* (this line spoken very softly).

apsar walakwena (in this and succeeding lines, quoted portions are
   generally slightly louder and higher in pitch).
wetarra.
e.   70
usu kunne.
wettar kunne.
etto napir."
"pe an takke moka.
anpamoka.   75
sa   apsala walakwen moka."
anna tare AAII.
key paynasae a.
"teysokku   melle   na kunnemarsunno a."
aha.
"ai nuet sao.   80
ai arkan kae ai."
ai arkan kasa.
pela.
perkusa.
mm.
e kwento   mai soke a.   85
achu sappuru e pokwa.
(laughs)
pela soke an ai.

Skins alone (in this and succeeding lines, quoted portions are generally
   slightly louder and higher in pitch).
Collared peccary.
Yes.   70
Agouti is eaten.
Collared peccary is eaten.
So indeed it is true."
(Turtle says) "You see me too.
Me also.   75
Shit   skin alone too."
Indeed we are equal FRIEND.
Nobody won ah.
"Therefore   we   will certainly not eat each other ah."
Aha.
"We will become good friends.   80
Friend let's shake hands friend."
The friends shook hands
That's the end.
It's finished.
Mm.
That is   the story ah.   85
Of Jungle Jaguar the two of them.
(Laughs)
That's the end I say my friend.

Figure 9. Monkey punches Turtle in the chest

Chapter 5

The Way of the Turtle

Told by Pedro Arias

Pedro Arias, then chief's spokesman of Mulatuppu, told *yarmoro ikar/ The Way of the Turtle* (as he called it) on the morning of June 29, 1970, in the Mulatuppu gathering house, during the annual celebration of the creation of the village school, an occasion on which he told several stories, including *The One-Eyed Grandmother.*[1] *The Way of the Turtle* is a relatively short story, opposing two protagonists, Turtle and Monkey.[2]

In this story, Monkey and Turtle go about tricking one another. This is unusual for a Kuna story in which it is typically the weaker of a pair of animals, for example, Agouti vs. Jaguar or Turtle vs. Jaguar, who tricks the stronger.[3] There are four episodes/tricks:

1. Monkey invites Turtle to eat food in his house in a tree but Turtle, because his feet (paws) are round, cannot climb up.

2. Turtle tricks Monkey into trying to clean his black hands (paws), as if they were dirty, before eating his (Turtle's) food, and he (Monkey) scrapes them. Furthermore, he burns himself touching the hot food.

3. Monkey hits Turtle and dents his chest, and that is how Turtle got the form he has.

4. Turtle hits Monkey with a stick in the nose and flattens it out, and that is how Monkey got that way.

Trickster stories, with humanlike animals, are a popular Kuna genre, as they are in many indigenous societies of the Americas. *The Way of the Turtle* is no doubt a Kuna version of a story or stories found elsewhere.[4] Turtle is a popular trickster. His exploits with Jaguar are depicted in chapter 4. The humor of this story derives from the very human and especially Kuna human aspects of the animals. They talk, they eat, and they carry on just like ordinary Kuna, including washing their hands carefully before eating. Some of the humor derives from the Kuna language and Kuna grammar. The animals are described as having hands and feet, like humans, rather than paws, like animals. But Turtle points out that he does not have claws (line 19) as Monkey does, and therefore cannot climb a tree, reminding the listeners that these characters are animals too. Pedro animates the characters in his performance of this story. He impersonates them by modulating and vibrating his voice with great gusto, alternating volume and speed, and shifting tempo. Repeated and onomatopoetic sounds and words mimic the actions and noises so crucial to the story and, along with the occasional use of a Spanish word, add to the expressive humor of the telling.

> They go along they go along they go along they go along they
>   go along (gets softer)   and fiiinally they geeet to his house.
> Smelling the food, Friend Monkey climbed *pioi pioi pioi pioi*
>   *pioi* (climbing noise), above.
> Friend   Friend Monkey said, "I'll wipe my paws ah."
> *Irki irki irki* (rubbing noise) to clean them in the water.
> *TAK*   in the chest here ah.
> He did it made a dent in the chest *SIII*
> See *negro* (Spanish) you see, dirty.

As in all Kuna storytelling, as well as chanting, body positions, explicitly expressed in verbs, add to the expressive detail as well as the humor of the performance.[5] Monkey is standing calling (line (16), just as monkeys do. And Turtle does not want anyone lying entering his food (line 39), a humorous way to describe eating, because turtles are always in a lying position. The story moves along quickly, with actions depicted and dialogue quoted.

The purpose of this story is humor and entertainment. The explanatory element is no doubt borrowed from elsewhere along with the story and provides one more ingredient of humor. And there is always a bit of moralizing that goes along with animal trickster tales, implicitly or explicitly: "Don't bicker and fight as these animals (and you) always do."

Olokwagdi de Akwanusadup's illustrations of Monkey punching Turtle (fig. 9) and Turtle hitting Monkey with a stick (fig. 10) capture the animal/human fusion of the characters. Their faces, actions, and imagined personalities are very human, with a suggestion, of course, of their animal features as well, including Turtle's shell and Monkey's tail. Monkey wears clothing; Turtle does not. The flowers, plants, and trees offer a stylized version of the Kuna jungle environment.

Here is the story.

Figure 10. Turtle hits Monkey with a stick

Kuna

takkarku   AI   ai   sur kamaitito sulu.
ai yarmoro epo.
ai yarmoroteka   emi e ai nuet ittolesunto, ai sur a.
tek ipakwenki   ai sur soysunna, "an aiye, an neyse mas kunnamaloye a.
mas nuet an imaysa takkenye."   5

teysokku, yarmoroto soysunna "kine,"   aipa.
ikarpa natapsunna, ai mas appan (voice vibrates) ittoe a.
"mas kunkuat appan" soysunto a.
natapsunna.
mas kunno ittole yarmoro pinsanatapsunto.   10
natap natap natap natap natap (gets softer)   peeekwache e nek
    oarrrmakkar.
mas appanne, ai surte nakkwichunnat pioi pioi pioi pioi pioi (climbing
    noise), nipa.
ai yarmorote, nak olor sokku, iki nakko a.
nipa key nakkwe kwer kwer kwer kwer (scratching noise), kunasunto.
kwenti surti tikka nipa tukku.   15
aise korkwichit "taye, mas kunta takke mas nuet siye."
wepa ai sur soy   ai yarmoro soysunna, "ai anki toto soy" sokeye.
"mak an takketteye a.
naymali konu satte.
nak ololet mak an takket, ai anki toto soy" soke soke.   20
napir soke.
suli a, arpisurkus a surtin, eti nanaerpat nipa tukku.
kannal aitenonito.
teki ai ai yarmoro sokku "napir" soke.
aika soysunna "tekir an aiye, ankat mas ittonamarmosunnoye a."   25
ai sur soke "napir" soke a.
sur natmosunto, yarmoro itutmokat.
sur sur sorpa nakusmosunto.
natap natap natap natap (gets softer) a ittonatapmosunna.
ai sur   ai yarmoro mas yappannet a.   30

English

So   FRIEND   Friend Monkey was going about Monkey was.
Friend Turtle the two of them.
And Friend Turtle   now and Friend Monkey it seems, are good friends
    ah.
Well one day   Friend Monkey says "My friend, let's go to my house to
    eat ah.
I made a good meal see."   5

Therefore, Turtle says "Ready,"   with his friend.
As they are going along the road, Friend smells the food (voice vibrates)
    ah.
"The food can be smelled" he said ah.
They are going along.
I am sure that I am going to eat Turtle thinks as he is going along.   10
They go along they go along they go along they go along they go along
    (gets softer)   and fiiinally they geeet to his house.
Smelling the food, Friend Monkey climbed *pioi pioi pioi pioi pioi*
    (climbing noise), above.
And Friend Turtle, since he has round feet, how could he climb up ah?
He cannot climb above *kwer kwer kwer kwer* (scratching noise), he
    kept doing it (scratching but not climbing).
But Monkey is above way up top.   15
 (Monkey) is standing calling his friend "Come, eat see there is good
    food."
That one Friend Monkey says   Friend Turtle says, "Friend you are
    making fun of me say" he says.
"I know what will happen.
I don't have claws.
Don't you see my feet are round, Friend you are making fun of me say"
    he says it is said.   20
It is true it is said.
No ah, he (Turtle) did not go ah that one did not go, but the other one
    is a climber up to the top.
He (Monkey) came down again.
Well Friend Turtle said "Alright" he says.
He says to his friend "Well my friend, let's go taste my food ah."   25
Friend Monkey says "Alright" he says ah.
Monkey went too, and Turtle also led the way.
Monkey Monkey was behind.
Going along going along going along going along (gets softer) ah they
    also smell as they go along.
Friend Monkey   Friend Turtle smells the food ah.   30
"It smells good" he (Monkey) said, "the food can be smelled" he

"yer appan" soysunto, "kunkuat ittole" soke.
peeekwache OARRMAA (derived from oarmakkar, but trails off, sounds
   like oarrmaa) takkar, mesa akkimai soysunto a.
mesaki pe takke masi tar tayleku takket ukakka, "ai mas   mas inso yer
   inso appan" soke.
"mas kunkuat" soysunto.
sikwitapsunto mesa nuet sii.   35
yarmoro sii, kwen simoka.
"kep" soytesunto yarmoro ai surkala.
"an ai surye   we an patte yakine, tule arkan chichikwa kwen
   otokosurye a.
arkan takutiymalatpi an maski otokemaiye.
maste ue ue palit.   40
ai surte arkan ulup korsulit a.
takken nekro pe takket, sippusulit.
ai   ai sur sokku, "arkan elie a."
irki irki irki tiki (rubbing noise) enuynasunnat.
irki irki irki.   45
takkusaeka teki kep "mas kunno" soket.
irki irki irki irki imaynasunto.
akkwa sip si irki irki irki irki arkan ulup YASA.
weki atarichunto a.
takku wis kusku," soyte "emiskinoye a."   50
achaten inikwen uerreket.
pule   nunmakke a.
pel aurmayte ittosa.
a sul iikkir imaysisunto annuyte.
IKKÍR   55
suli maskuchasurkusmoka.
peeche.
"yartaylesmosunto.
na tarre na oyartaysat."
kep asorpa ai sur soysunna.   60

"yarmoro anki totoe."
a, napir soke.
kep epo ali   kep immaysasunto, pinale   immaysa TAK   pinaskarki
   weki a.
imma pinaskar kure SII
yarmoro ittos.   65
"weki pe kate kuakatye"   kar soytesunto ai surte a.
yarmoroka.
"wey pe kateku yarkan   wey pe pinaskar kure pe katkuo takkenye."

(Monkey) says.

Fiiinally they GET THERE see, with the table full of food it is said ah.

On the table you see there are indeed see many kinds of food, "Friend the
    food   the food therefore smells   therefore good" he says.

"The food can be smelled" he said.

They went and sat down on a good bench that was there.   35

Turtle is sitting, the other is sitting also.

"Well" said Turtle to Friend Monkey.

"My friend Monkey   I don't want anyone, with black (= dirty) hands
    to enter (= eat) inside my plate ah.

Only those with whitish (= clean) hands can be lying entering (= eating)
    my food."

And the food was hot hot too.   40

And Friend Monkey has dirty palms.

See *negro* (black) you see, dirty.

Friend   Friend Monkey said, "I'll wipe my paws ah."

Irki irki irki (rubbing noise) to clean them in the water.

Irki irki irki.   45

In order to make them whitish well then "Let's eat" he says.

Irki irki irki irki he kept doing it.

With a white stone that was there *irki irki irki irki* his palm *YASA*
    (expressive word).

Here he tore it ah.

"It got a little whitish," he said "now then ah."   50

Barely had he touched it (the food) right away it's hot.

It hurts   a lot ah.

He got all scorched did you hear?

Ah Monkey pulled back he did he touched.

IKKÍR (expressive word).   55

No he could not eat either (because his hand hurt).

Wow.

"I was tricked also.

Now we're tied at being tricked."

Then afterwards Friend Monkey says.   60

"Turtle is tricking me."

Ah, it is true it is said.

Then they both came together   then he (Monkey) did it (hit him), softly
    he did it *TAK*   in the chest here ah.

He did it made a dent in the chest *SIII* (expressive word).

To the Turtle did you hear.   65

"You will always be like this"   he said to him Friend Monkey did ah.

To Turtle.

"You will always be like this your back   here your chest will always be
    dented see."

kep, wepa yarmoro soytesunna "anki totokosurye"   kep
  suar amismosunto.
aypiliar imaysa   TAK suarki asu.   70
asu silir SImoka.
"weki pe katkumo takken" kar soysunna.
"weki pe tatalet kumokoye."
teysokku aula   yarmoro   pinaskar kure kusye.
ai sur   yarmoro imasmo aula asu silir kusmo takken soysunto.   75
we teki saylakine   nek kustakkenye   yarmoroye ikar ma soysunto
  ittosa.
we ikar tey ma soysunto.
pittokua.
ati tesepa.
anna.   80

Then, he Turtle said "(You) will not joke with me"   then he (Turtle)
    got a stick.
When he (Monkey) turned around he did it (gave it to him)   *TAK*
    (expressive word) with the stick in the nose.   70
He HAS a flattened out nose.
"This is the way you'll always be also see" he says to him.
"This is the way you will be when you become a grandfather."
Therefore thus   Turtle   got a dented chest.
Friend Monkey   Turtle also did it to him thus he got a flat nose see
    it is said.   75
Here well in olden times   is what happened   it is the way of the
    Turtle it is said did you hear.
This way is like this it is said.
Did you hear.
Up to here.
So there.   80

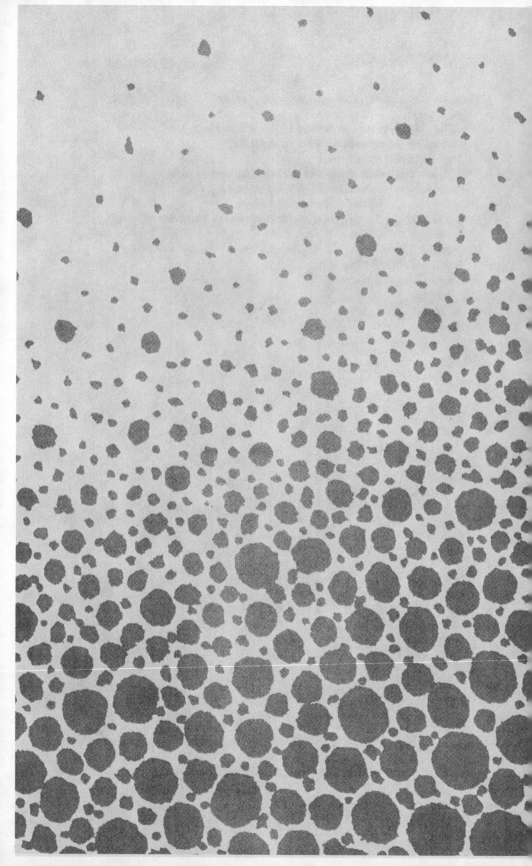

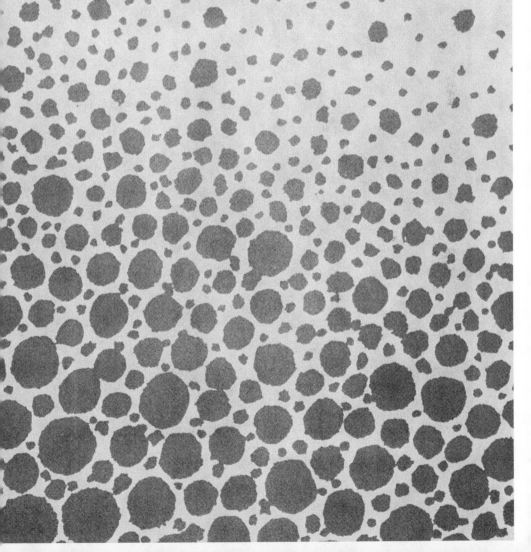

PART II

Myths and
Magical Chants

Figure 11. *Counseling the way of the devil medicine*

Chapter 6

Counsel to the Way of the Devil Medicine

Performed by Anselmo Urrutia

Nia ikar ina unae/Counsel to the Way of the Devil Medicine was performed by Anselmo Urrutia in a house in Panama City in 1998. Anselmo Urrutia came from a family of political leaders and ritual specialists. His father was a chief and curing specialist and died when Anselmo was very young. Anselmo was taken care of by his older brother, Olowiktinappi, also a curing specialist. It is Olowiktinappi who performed *The Way of Rattlesnake*, which is represented in this book.[1] Anselmo Urrutia died on February 21, 2003, at the age of eighty-five. While Anselmo did not know any long curing chants, he was a specialist in medicinal plants and knew and performed medicine counsels, such as *Counsel to the Way of the Devil Medicine*.[2] He was my assistant and close collaborator in the study of Kuna language and culture for many years.

Counsel to the Way of the Devil Medicine is used, along with appropriate medicinal plants, and a much longer chant, *nia ikar /The Way of the Devil* in order to cure a person who is mentally deranged.[3] It is addressed to the spirits of the medicine that will be used in the cure. It shares features with other medicine counsels and curing chants more generally, in particular, it demonstrates verbally to the spirits that the chanter knows their origins, and with them the origins of the special plants that constitute the medicine, and can thus control them. Once a patient has been diagnosed as needing devil medicine, specialists like Anselmo Urrutia gather it in the jungle and perform *Counsel to the Way of the Devil Medicine* to it.

STRUCTURE OF CHANT

Counsel to the Way of the Devil Medicine is short and charmlike. Throughout, as in all medicine counsels, there is constant repetition, in parallel lines, of the task at hand, to clear away evil spirits, in this case, the spirit of the devil, with the assistance of the medicine. In particular, the lines "Sacred medicine(s) you are being counseled" and "There are many (live) sacred uncle (devils)" are repeated over and over, conferring an incantatory tone on the delivery. The struggle between the spirit of the medicine and the spirit of the devil is described as a battle between the medicine and his troops and the devil and his troops, all taking place within the spirit world. The fermented drink chicha is used as an element in the battle. The medicine wins out, and the real, live, human patient is thus cured. It is interesting to note that the evil spirit, the devil, is also sacred, and while the goal is to eliminate him, he is treated with respect.

As in all curing and magical chants, there is a special vocabulary, the esoteric, ritual, metaphorical lexicon of the spirit world. A good example is *tona ipekkwa* "owner of tobacco" (which in other chants is *inna ipekkwa* "owner of chicha"), which signifies *tule* "Kuna person." This esoteric metaphor is based on two of the most ritual, sacred items in Kuna life, native tobacco, which is used in curing ceremonies, to smoke out evil spirits, and the fermented drink chicha, which is consumed at young girls' puberty rites and is also used as an element of battle against evil spirits.

The medicine is counseled to work for four days, a temporal expression that is stated in esoteric words. Four is the most sacred Kuna number, especially in curing chants, which, along with associated medicine, are usually performed for four days. *Posumpa* is an esoteric word used in curing chants to mean house; I translate it here as "abode." *Totokkwa* is an esoteric word meaning "small"; I translate it here as "tiny." The nominal prefix *po* and the verbal suffixes *yola*, *ini*, and *kwa* are all part of the ritual language of curing chants. Many lines end in the suffix *-ye*, as is common in curing and magical chants. Most morphemes, especially nouns and verbs and their suffixes, occur in their long form, which includes a final vowel, contrasting sharply with everyday and informal speech, in which these vowels are typically deleted.

Counsel to the Way of the Devil Medicine works because of the belief by the performer, his patient, and the entire Kuna community in its efficacy, in the power of humans to control spirits by means of chants such as this one.

Olokwagdi de Akwanusadup's imaginative illustration, *Counseling the Way of the Devil Medicine* (fig. 11), shows a medicinal specialist, such as Anselmo Urrutia, wearing a hat with a feather, a traditional sign of his profession, concentrating as he chants to the medicine he has gathered, now in a Kuna basket, to ward off the shadowy spirit of the devil, which is attacking the sick individual. This individual is depicted as intermediate between the human world of the chanter and the dark spirit world of the devil. This illustration, like the chant, depicts the intimate communication between the performer and the plant medicine through the mediation of the spirit world. My photograph (photo 4) shows Anselmo Urrutia listening to the recording of his performance.

Here is the *Counsel to the Way of the Devil Medicine.*

Kuna

tulalele na pe uanaye.
sia unae emar moka (said to Joel Sherzer).
patto tioleleti nuitakketi ipa pe tulekwa opinnitemala.
tulalelekan na pe uanaye.
tulalelerpaye pani tarpa tar piyekwayola.
tulalelerpa pani tarpa tar sokekuteye.   5
ani tona ipekkwatinaye.
kilulele niakkwalelekante.
se iwala maiye pi takke sokele.
teeti iwala opurrekala.
tulalele nakaye tar pe uanae.   10
ani tona ipekkwa naye.
kilulele mai tolakante.
se iwala maiye pi takke sokele.
teeti iwala ekwaneye.
tulalele nakaye tar pe uanaeye.   15
patto tiolele.
weki tona ipekan.
kilulele mai tolakanase iwala makkitemalatteyeti, iwala opurre pe peeti
    ulale.
patto tioleleti pe tulakwa opinnitemala.
tulelelekan na pe uanaemala.   20
iki tona ipekkwate pali penesuenaesuli pali tar kuemala silakwaye.
ipalelekana pali penesutemalatti, tulalele pani tarpa tarpiyekwayola.
ipa nuchu nelekana pali penetaytemalatti, tulalele pani tarpa
    tarpiyekwayola.
teeti pakkakwa yopi.
tona ipekkwate pali penesuenaemala.   25
iki tona ipekkwaki pali pannakuenaemala teeye kepe ipi tar sokekuteye.
tulalele pani tarpakwa sokekuteye.
kilulele mai tolakan.
iwala ekwanekala, iwala opurrekala.
kilulele mai tolakana.   30
iki tona ipekkwase iwala mai yepi, mai yepie pali tar pee pukkwamalat
    teeye kepe ipi tar sokekuteye.
tona ipekkwa.
kilulele mai tolakante.
iki se iwala maiye pi pali kuepie naka tar pali pee pukkwamalateye kepe
    ipi tar sokekuteye.
ipekala kwinpakke naakwale.   35
tona ipekkwa pokachi ulupa neka kunitto nikkimalinye.
kilulele mai tolakantu.
ipekala kwinpakke naakwale.

English

Sacred medicine you are being counseled.
It's like the cocoa counsel (said to Joel Sherzer).
In the beginning one day sacred god transformed to his liking your live
    being.
Sacred medicines you are being counseled.
You know all about medicine it is sounded.
You know all about medicine it is said.   5
And my owner of tobacco (Kuna person).
There are many sacred uncle devils.
Who have come to his path see it is said.
In order to mix up the path.
Sacred medicine you are being counseled.   10
My owner of tobacco.
There are many live sacred uncles.
Who have come to his path see it is said.
To gather them away from the path.
Sacred medicine you are being counseled.   15
In the beginning sacred god.
Owners of tobacco who are here.
Sacred uncle always comes to the path, for this reason you must mix up
    the path.
In the beginning sacred god transformed your live being.
Sacred medicines you are being counseled.   20
How can we not help the owner of tobacco again as we always do.
Sacred prophets you have been helpers before, sacred medicine you must
    do it again.
Small prophets you have been helpers before, sacred medicine you must
    do it again.
You are the knowers.
You must go again to help the owner of tobacco.   25
How could we depart from the owner of tobacco again then it is said.
Sacred medicine you know many diseases it is said.
There are many live sacred uncles.
In order to gather them away from the path, in order to mix up the path.
There are many live sacred uncles.   30
That they do not come again, to the path of the owner of tobacco then it
    is said.
Owner of tobacco.
There are many live sacred uncles.
That they do not come again to his path then it is said.
For four days you will work.   35
Under the ritual hammock of the owner of tobacco you will protect him.
Against live sacred uncles.
For four days.

tona ipekkwa pokachi ulupa, purpalele opinyekwanaesemalainiye.
kilulele mai tolakantu.   40
kilulele mai tolakantu.
iki tona ipekkwase iwala maiye nae pali kuepie naka tar pali pee
    pukkwamalatteye.
tona ipekkwa pali penesutemalatteye.
pani sailakanse aitete pani kutemaloe.
inna kuakwale sailakanse upote pani kutemaloe.   45
iki tona ipekkwaki pali pannakuenaemalateye, kepe ipi tar sokekuteye.
tulalele naka tar pe uanae.
pela uanayakwele.
pani neka kunitto nikkimalainiye.
tona ipekkwa.   50
posumpa totokkwa alimakkekwayola.
kilulele tarpa pulekantu iniye.
kilulele tarpa pulekante.
tona ipekkwase kala kwen imakkepi takke sokele.
tee yeti iwala ekwane.   55
tee yeti ali sokenae.
tulalekan nakase na pe uanae.

Under the ritual hammock of the owner of tobacco, you will transform
   his sacred soul.
Against live sacred uncles.   40
Against live sacred uncles.
That he does not come again to the path of the owner of tobacco.
The owner of tobacco's helpers again.
You will descend to your chiefs you will.
You will carry some chicha to your chiefs you will.   45
How could we depart from the owner of tobacco again, then it is said.
Sacred medicine you are being counseled.
All is being counseled.
You must be there protecting.
The owner of tobacco.   50
The tiny abode is full (of medicine).
In front of sacred uncle and the other valiant ones.
There are many sacred uncles and valiant ones.
So that different kinds (of evil spirits) do not come to the owner of
   tobacco see it is said.
To gather them away from his path.   55
Come to help it is said.
Sacred medicines you are being counseled.

Figure 12. Counseling the cooling off spirits

Chapter 7

The Way of Cooling Off

Performed by Pranki Pilos

Tampoet ikar/The Way of Cooling Off was performed by Pranki Pilos in his home in Mulatuppu on December 10, 1978. Pranki Pilos was a specialist in medicine, both herbal and therapeutic. He was especially known for his remarkable ability to learn and perform long, memorized chants. Among those he knew were *The Way of the Hot Pepper, The Way of Sweet Basil, The Way of the Wasp, The Way of the Snake,*[1] and *The Way of Cooling Off.* At the end of his life, he learned the very long, powerful, and important *The Way of Balsa Wood,* used for the prevention and cure of epidemics and epidemic-like sicknesses and problems, which is performed over a several day period.

The Way of Cooling Off is used to cool and calm a baby with a high fever. It is performed to a set of plant spirits who, by a kind of symbolic/sympathetic magic, due to their physical and spiritual properties, essentially coolness and coldness, cool down the fever of the baby. A remarkable knowledge of the plant world and spirit names for it are reflected and expressed in this text. The naming of the spirits is essential to their efficacy. The performance of the chant counsels the spirits and causes them to gather and to descend to the body of the patient and cure him or her.

The overriding and constantly reiterated theme of this chant, expressed both explicitly and metaphorically, is coolness. The places, objects, spirits, and moments named are all associated with coolness. Mountains, lakes, rivers, plants, and the rising of the sun are all very poetically described and evoked and are all aimed at enacting and achieving the cooling off of the baby's fever.

STRUCTURE OF CHANT

The Way of Cooling Off is a mosaic of incantatory and soothing repetitions and parallelisms. This structure is an important aspect of its length and efficacy. After an introduction in which each spirit is named and counseled to come into action, a basic verse pattern is repeated, each time naming a different body part of the sick baby and asking the spirits to cool them off or otherwise calm and cure them. Here is the verse pattern, which begins with soul and successively then names body fluid (= blood), clothes (= skin), body, brain, hair, chicha path (= throat), and vision (= eyes):

> Indeed they are in place in their abode they are watching over
>   their abode.
> They are making their abode cool.
> Indeed they are really learning about the patient.
> Our owner of chicha's little one (the Kuna person's baby).
> His soul is very feverish.
> Be cooling off his soul again for him.
> Really making his soul cool again.

In addition to this repeated verse structure, lines and groups of lines are repeated throughout the text. Examples are:

> At the place of the rising sun.
> The Cooling Off People spouses.
> Are truly beginning to be called.

> The Cooling Off People spouses come and descend.
> All very cold very cold.

> Your tiny seeds are falling.
> On top of the boulders.

The chant ends with a coda or conclusion, which sums up what the chant knower and performer, Pranki Pilos, wants the spirits to do:

> The spirits are calling out the specialist is also calling out.
> Now that all the Cooling Off People spouses have gathered.

Now that all the Cooling Off People spouses have gathered.
The spirits are also calling out.

Up to every part of them.
Up to the last part of them.
All of the Cooling Off People spouses are in place.
Now that they have come to the specialist.

And our owner of chicha's little one.
After four days and nights.
He will be bathed with you (the plants whose spirits have been
    counseled).
The spirits are all counseled.
You who truly know.
Spirits you are indeed counseled.

The Kuna concept of counsel, verbally enacted through the power of words, is crucial to the efficacy and success of this chant. The chant knower summons the spirits to a meeting, remarkably like the meetings real, human Kuna have every day. And just as real, human Kuna are counseled by their chiefs and other leaders to cooperate in the achievement of a task at hand, the spirits and their spouses are counseled to carry out the cure of the patient.

VOCABULARY, GRAMMAR, AND STYLE

There is a special, esoteric language that is used in *The Way of Cooling Off*, as in all Kuna magical and curing chants. The vocabulary is both metaphorical and playful. Here are some examples: The Kuna person is called "the owner of chicha," the fermented drink consumed at the very important puberty ritual for young girls; the baby is called "the little one"; the baby's skin is called "clothes"; his/her throat is called "the chicha path." In general, I have tried to match Kuna esoteric or poetic words with English ones. Thus I have used "spouse" for woman, "vision" for eyes, "patient" for sick person, and "breeze" for wind. The ritual language of this text is distinct from but translatable into everyday Kuna. It is the language of the spirits, who understand it when it is performed to them in chants like *The Way of Cooling Off*. Particularly important in this regard is the naming of the spirits in their own secret language. This demonstrates to them that the chant knower is familiar with them and their properties and convinces them to do his bidding.

As is typical in curing and magical chanting, forms in this performance of *The Way of Cooling Off* usually contain the final vowel that is deleted in everyday speech. Lines usually end in the suffix -*ye*. Both of these features contribute to this chant's incantatory quality.

The text of *The Way of Cooling Off* is fixed and must be memorized word by word. Individual variations occur in actual performance with regard to pause, pitch, and musical patterning and therefore in the structuring of lines and verses. The form of certain verbal suffixes sometimes varies as well. In his performance, Pranki Pilos creates miniature tensions and counterpoints between the basic structure of this fixed text and tiny variations here and there.

Olokwagdi de Akwanusadup's illustration *Counseling the Cooling Off Spirits* (fig. 12) shows a medicinal specialist, such as Pranki Pilos, seated in front of a hammock in which is lying a sick child. Under the hammock is a box of wooden *nuchus* "stick dolls," which are representatives of the spirits of good whom the specialist is counseling to cure the child. At the top of the illustration, watching over all this, is an outline of a Kuna woman, perhaps the spirit of the mother of the child, perhaps *nan tummat*, the "great mother" of all Kuna. The specialist is concentrating all his attention on the stick dolls with whom he is communicating. My photograph (photo 5) shows Pranki Pilos seated in his home, with his staff, beads, and tie, all signs of his profession.

Here is *The Way of Cooling Off*, as performed by Pranki Pilos.

Figure 13. Chanting to the chicha

Kuna

waiye.[2]
nekati ainakkwaye neka paliye.
tammipa tola walepunkanse.
sunna okolemekwialiye.

punati inati aktukkwaliyopi walepunkanse sunna okoletakeye.

tammipa tola walepunkan aiteketakeye.   5

pel apa tammipale tammipalepiye.

na kalupi kaenai kalu etarpenai.
kalu tammipamakkenaiye.
na pinakinet wisikuenaiye.

nekati ainakkwaye neka paliye.   10
tammipa tola walepunkanse sunna okolemaiye.
puna inati aktukkwaliyopi walepunkan aiteketakeye.
pel apa tammipale tammipalepiye.

na kalupi kaenai kalu etarpenaiye.
kalu tammipamakkenaiye.   15
na pinakinet wisikuekwanaiye.

an inna ipekkwa yapakilakkwati.
ka purpa uemaytemalattiye.
ka purpati pali tampokenai.
purpa pali tammipamakkekwanaiye.   20

an inna ipekkwa yapakilakkwati apalisa ueletetiye.
apalis uemaytemalattiye.
ka apalis pali tampokenai.
apalis pali tammipamakkekwanaiye.

an inna ipekkwa yapakilakkwatina.   25
ka mola ueletemalatti.
mola uemaytemalattiye.
ka molati pali tampokenai.
mola pali tammipamakkekwanaiye.

English

waiye.[2]
At the place of the rising sun.
The Cooling Off People spouses.
Are truly beginning to be called.

The Sister Sacred Aktukkwaliyopi (name of medicinal plant that grows in
    river) spouses truly come and are called.

The Cooling Off People spouses come and descend.   5

All very cold very cold.

Indeed they are in place in their abode they are watching over their
    abode.
They are making their abode cool.
Indeed they are learning about the patient.

At the place of the rising sun.   10
The Cooling Off People spouses are truly being called.
The Sister Sacred Aktukkwaliyopi spouses come and descend.
All very cold very cold.

Indeed they are in place in their abode they are watching over their
    abode.
They are making their abode cool.   15
Indeed they are really learning about the patient.

Our owner of chicha's little one (the Kuna person's baby).
His soul is very feverish.
Be cooling off his soul again for him.
Really making his soul cool again.   20

Our owner of chicha's little one's body fluid (blood) has become feverish.
His body fluid is very feverish.
Be cooling off his body fluid again for him.
Really making his body fluid cool again.

And our owner of chicha's little one.   25
His clothes (skin) have become very feverish.
His clothes are very feverish.
Be cooling off his clothes again for him.
Really making his clothes cool again.

an inna ipekkwa yapakilakkwakalaye. 30
ka apakan ueletemalattiye.
apakana uemaytemalattiye.
ka apakan pali tampokenai.
apakan pali tammipamakkekwanaiye.

an inna ipekkwa yapakilakkwakala. 35
ka kurkin ueletemalattiye.
ka kurkin uemaytemalattiye.
ka kurkina pali tampokenanaiye.
ka kurkin pali tammipamakkekwanaiye.

an inna ipekkwa yapakilakkwakala. 40
ka sayliki ueletemalatti.
ka sayliki uemaytemalattiye.
ka saylikiti pali tampokenai.
sayliki pali tammipamakkekwanaiye.

an inna ipekkwa yapakilakkwaka. 45
ka inna iawala kialeteti.
iawar kiamaytemalatti.
ka iawar pal ekaenai.
iawar pali tutturmakkenaiye.

an inna ipekkwa yapakilakkwakala. 50
ka tala itsotemalatti.
tala momomaytemalatti.
ka tala pali kannokenanai.
ka tala pali tutturmakkekwanaiye.

nekati ainakkwa neka pali. 55
ti tukku tola walepunkanse sunna na okolemekwialiye.
puna inati nusaktitili walepunkan aitealiye.
pel apa tammipalepi.
tammipalepi   na walepunkan aiteketake.

na kalupi kaenai kalu etarpenai. 60
kalu tammipamakkenaiye.
na pinakinet wisikuenaiye.

nekati ainakkwa neka pali.
ti tukku tola walepunkanse sunna okoletakeye.
puna inati nusaktitili walepunkan aiteketakeye. 65

Our owner of chicha's little one.   30
His body has become very feverish.
His body is very feverish.
Be cooling off his body again for him.
Really making his body cool again.

Our owner of chicha's little one.   35
His brain has become very feverish.
His brain is very feverish.
Be cooling off his brain again for him.
Really making his brain cool again for him.

Our owner of chicha's little one.   40
His hair has become very feverish.
His hair is very feverish.
Be cooling off his hair again for him.
Really making his hair cool again.

Our owner of chicha's little one.   45
His chicha path (throat) has become clogged.
His path is very clogged.
Be opening his path again for him.
Making his path straight again.

Our owner of chicha's little one.   50
His vision has become very damaged.
His vision has very much dwindled.
Be strengthening his vision again for him.
Really making his vision straight again for him.

At the place of the rising sun.   55
The River Source People spouses are indeed truly beginning to be called.
The Sister Sacred Nusaktitili (name of medicinal stone found in rivers)
    spouses begin to descend.
All very cold.
Very cold   indeed the spouses come and descend.

Indeed they are in place in their abode they are watching over their
    abode.   60
They are making their abode cool.
Indeed they are learning about the patient.

At the place of the rising sun.
The River Source People spouses truly come and are called.
The Sister Sacred Nusaktitili spouses come and descend.   65

pel apa tammipalepiye.
walepunkan aiteketake.

na kalupi kaenai kalu etarpenai.
kalu tammipamakkenaiye.
na pinakinet wisikuekwanaiye.   70

an inna ippekkwa yapakilakkwaka purpa ueletemalatti.
ka purpa uemaytemalattikwaye.
ka purpati pali tampokenanaiye.
ka purpa pali tammipamakkekwanaiye.

an inna ipekkwa yapakilakkwakalaye.   75
apalisa ueletemalattiye.
apalis uemaytemalattikwaye.
ka apalis pali tampokenanaiye.
ka apalis pali tammipamakkekwanaiye.

an inna ipekkwa yapakilakkwakalaye.   80
ka mola ueletemalattiye.
ka mola uemaytemalattikwaye.
ka molati pali tampokenai.
mola pali tammipamakkekwanaiye.

an inna ipekkwa yapakilakkwakalainiye.   85
ka apakan ueletemalattiye.
ka apakan uemaytemalattikwaye.
ka apakan pali tampokenanaiye.
apakan pali tammipamakkekwanaiye.

an inna ipekkwa yapakilakkwakalaye.   90
ka kurkin ueletemalatti.
kurkin uemaytemalattiye.
kurkina pali tampokenanaiye.
kurkin pali tammipamakkekwanaiye.

an inna ipekkwa yapakilakkwakala.   95
sayliki ueletemalatti.
sayliki uetetemalatti.
ka sayliki pali tampokenai.
sayliki pali tammipamakkekwanaiye.

an inna ipekkwa yapakilakkwakala.   100
inna iawala kialete.
inna iawar kiamaytemalat.

All very cold.
The spouses come and descend.

Indeed they are in place in their abode they are watching over their
    abode.
They are making their abode cool.
Indeed they are really learning about the patient.   70

Our owner of chicha's little one's soul has become very feverish.
His soul is very feverish.
Be cooling off his soul again for him.
Really making his soul cool again for him.

Our owner of chicha's little one.   75
His body fluid has become very feverish.
His body fluid is very feverish.
Be cooling off his body fluid again for him.
Really making his body fluid cool again for him.

Our owner of chicha's little one.   80
His clothes have become very feverish.
His clothes are very feverish.
Be cooling off his clothes again for him.
Really making his clothes cool again.

Our owner of chicha's little one.   85
His body has become very feverish.
His body is very feverish.
Be cooling off his body again for him.
Really making his body cool again.

Our owner of chicha's little one.   90
His brain has become very feverish.
His brain is very feverish.
Be cooling off his brain again.
Really making his brain cool again.

Our owner of chicha's little one.   95
His hair has become very feverish.
His hair is very feverish.
Be cooling off his hair again for him.
Really making his hair cool again.

Our owner of chicha's little one.   100
His chicha path has become clogged.
His chicha path is very clogged.

ka iawar pal ekaenai.
iawala pali tutturmakkekwanaiye.

an inna ipekkwa yapakilakkwakalaye.   105
ka tala itsotemalatti.
tala momomaytemalatti.
tala pali kannokenanai.
tala pali   tutturmakkekwanaiye.

nekati ainakkwaye neka pali ti tukku tola.   110
walepunkanse sunna na okolemekwialiye.
puna inati aylitiryaisopiye.
walepunkan aiteketakeye.

pela apa tammipale tammipalepi.
walepunkan aiteketakeye.   115

na kalupi kaenai kalu etarpenai.
kalu tammipamakkekwanaiye.
na pinakinet wisikuenaiye.

nekati ainakkwaye neka pali tammipa tola walepunkanse sunna
    okolemekwialiye.

puna inati aylitiryaisopi walepunkan aiteketakeye.   120
pel apa tammipalepiye.
walepunkan aiteketakeye.

na kalupi kaenai kalu etarpenai.
kalu tammipamakkekwanaiye.
pinakinet wisikuenaiye.   125

an inna ipekkwa yapakilakkwakala.
ka purpa ueletemalatti.
ka purpa uemaytemala.
ka purpati pali tampokenanai.
purpa pali tammipamakkekwanaiye.   130

an inna ipekkwa yapakilakkwakalaye.
apalisa ueletemalatti.
apalis uemaytemalattikwa.
apalis pali tampokenai.
apalis pali tammipamakkekwanaiye.   135

Be opening his path again for him.
Really making his path straight again.

Our owner of chicha's little one.   105
His vision has become very damaged.
His vision has very much dwindled.
Be strengthening his vision again.
Really making his vision   straight again.

At the place of the rising sun the River Source People.   110
Spouses are indeed truly beginning to be called.
The Sister Sacred Aylitiryaisopi (name of small mangrove [medicinal
   plant] that grows in river).
Spouses come and descend.

All very cold very cold.
The spouses come and descend.   115

Indeed they are in place in their abode they are watching over their
   abode.
They are really making their abode cool.
Indeed they are learning about the patient.

At the place of the rising sun the Cooling Off People spouses are truly
   being called.

The Sister Sacred Aylitiryaisopi spouses come and descend.   120
All very cold.
The spouses come and descend.

Indeed they are in place in their abode they are watching over their
   abode.
They are really making their abode cool.
They are learning about the patient.   125

Our owner of chicha's little one.
His soul has become very feverish.
His soul is very feverish.
Be cooling off his soul again for him.
Really making his soul cool again.   130

Our owner of chicha's little one.
His body fluid has become very feverish.
His body fluid is very feverish.
Be cooling off his body fluid again.
Really making his body fluid cool again.   135

an inna ipekkwa yapakilakkwakalaye.
ka mola ueletemalatti.
mola uemaytemalatti.
ka molati pali tampokenaiye.
mola pali tammipamakkekwanaiye.   140

an inna ipekkwa yapakilakkwakala.
apakan ueletemalattiye.
apakan uemaytemalattiye.

ka apakan pali tampokenanai.
apakan pali tammipamakkekwanaiye.   145

an inna ipekkwa yapakilakkwakala.
kurkin ueletemalatti.
kurkin uemaytemala.
ka kurkina pali tampokenai.
kurkin pali tammipamakkekwanaiye.   150

an inna ipekkwa yapakilakkwakalaye.
ka sayliki ueletemalatti.
sayliki uemaytemalattiye.
ka sayliki pali tampokenai.
sayliki pali tammipamakkekwanaiye.   155

an inna ipekkwa yapakilakkwakalaye.
ka inna iawala kialete.
iawar kiamaytemalattiye.

ka iawar pal ekaenai.
iawala pali tutturmakkekwanaiye.   160

an inna ipekkwa yapakilakkwakala.
ka tala itsotemalatti.
tala tar kakatemalattikwaye.
ka tala pali kannokenanaiye.

nekati ainakkwaye neka paliye.   165
tammipa tola walepunkanse sunna okolemaiye.

puna inati nakkitili walepunkanse sunna okoletakeye.

tammipa tola walepunkan aiteketakeye pel apa tammipalepiye.

Our owner of chicha's little one.
His clothes have become very feverish.
His clothes are very feverish.
Be cooling off his clothes again for him.
Really making his clothes cool again.   140

Our owner of chicha's little one.
His body has become very feverish.
His body is very feverish.

Be cooling off his body again for him.
Really making his body cool again.   145

Our owner of chicha's little one.
His brain has become very feverish.
His brain is very feverish.
Be cooling off his brain again for him.
Really making his brain cool again.   150

Our owner of chicha's little one.
His hair has become very feverish.
His hair is very feverish.
Be cooling off his hair again for him.
Really making his hair cool again.   155

Our owner of chicha's little one.
His chicha path has become clogged.
His path is very clogged.

Be opening his path again for him.
Really making his path straight again.   160

Our owner of chicha's little one.
His vision has become very damaged.
His vision seems very misty.
Be strengthening his vision again for him.

At the place of the rising sun.   165
The Cooling Off People spouses are truly being called.

The Sister Sacred Nakkitili (name of a medicinal plant) spouses truly
    come and are called.

The Cooling Off People spouses come and descend all very cold.

na kalupi kaenai kalu etarpenai.
kalu tammipamakkekwanaiye.   170

pinakinet wisikuekwanaiye.

pa wini sakki tirpa ulu arpatyekwici.
ipe nuselupillisekaye.

an inna ipekkwa yapakilakkwakalaye.
ka purpa ueletemalatti.   175
purpa uemaytemalatti.
ka purpati pali tampokenai purpa pali.
tammipamakkekwanaiye.

an inna ipekkwaa yapakilakkwakalaye.
ka apalisa ueletemalatti.   180
apalis uemaytemalattiye.
ka apalis pali tampokenai.
apalis pali tammipamakkekwanai.

an inna ipekkwa yapakilakkwakala.
ka mola ueletemalattiye.   185
mola uemaytemalattiye.

ka molati pali tampokenanai.
mola pali tammipamakkekwanaiye.

an inna ipekkwa yapakilakkwakala.
ka apakan ueletemalatti.   190
apakan uemaytemalattiye.

ka apakan pali tampokenanai.
apakan pali tammipamakkekwanaiye.

an inna ipekkwa yapakilakkwakala.
ka kurkin ueletemalatti.   195
kurkin uemaytemalattiye.

ka kurkina pali tampokenai.
kurkin pali tammipamakkekwanaiye.

an inna ipekkwa yapakilakkwaka.
ka sayliki ueletemalatti.   200
sayliki uemaytemalattiye.

Indeed they are in place in their abode they are watching over their
   abode.
They are really making their abode cool.   170

They are really learning about the patient.

Your tiny seeds are falling.
On top of the boulders.

Our owner of chicha's little one.
His soul has become very feverish.   175
His soul is very feverish.
Be cooling off his soul again for him his soul again.
Really making it cool.

Our owner of chicha's little one.
His body fluid has become very feverish.   180
His body fluid is very feverish.
Be cooling off his body fluid again for him.
Really making his body fluid cool again.

Our owner of chicha's little one.
His clothes have become very feverish.   185
His clothes are very feverish.

Be cooling off his clothes again for him.
Really making his clothes cool again.

Our owner of chicha's little one.
His body has become very feverish.   190
His body is very feverish.

Be cooling off his body again for him.
Really making his body cool again.

Our owner of chicha's little one.
His brain has become very feverish.   195
His brain is very feverish.

Be cooling off his brain again for him.
Really making his brain cool again.

Our owner of chicha's little one.
His hair has become very feverish.   200
His hair is very feverish.

ka sayliki pali tampokenai.
sayliki pali tammipamakkekwanai.

an inna ipekkwa yapakilakkwakala.
inna iawala kialeteye.   205
inna iawar kiamaytemalat.

iawar pal ekaenai.
iawar pali tutturmakkekwanaiye.

an inna ipekkwa yapakilakkwakala.
ka tala itsotemalatti.   210
tala tar kakatemalattiye.

tala pali kannokenanai.
tala pali tutturmakkekwanaiye.

nekati ainakkwaye neka paliye.
tammipa tola walepunkanseye.   215
sunna na okolemekwisa.

puna inati sikkitili walepunkana aiteketakeye.
pel apa tammipale tammipalepi.
walepunkan aitekekwa.
na kalupi kaenai kalu etarpenai.   220
kalu tammipamakkekwanai.
na pinakinet wisikuali.

pe wini sakki tirpa ulu arpatyekwiciye.
ipe nuselupilliseye.

nekati ainakkwaye neka pali.   225
tammipa tola walepunkanse sunna okolemai.

puna inati sikkitili walepunkan aiteketake.
pel apa tammipale tammipalepiye.
walepunkan aiteketake.

na kalupi kaenai kalu etarpenai.   230
kalu tammipamakkekwanaiye.

pinakinet wisikuekwanaiye.

Be cooling off his hair again for him.
Really making his hair cool again.

Our owner of chicha's little one.
His chicha path has become clogged. 205
His chicha path is very clogged.

Be opening his path again.
Really making his path straight again.

Our owner of chicha's little one.
His vision has become very damaged. 210
His vision seems very misty.

Be strengthening his vision again.
Really making his vision straight again.

At the place of the rising sun.
The Cooling Off People spouses. 215
Are indeed truly being called.

The Sister Sacred Sikkitili (name of small calabash, a medicinal plant)
    spouses come and descend.
All very cold very cold.
The spouses really descend.
Indeed they are in place in their abode they are watching over their
    abode. 220
They are really making their abode cool.
Indeed they are learning about the patient.

Your tiny seeds are falling.
On top of the boulders.

At the place of the rising sun. 225
The Cooling Off People spouses are truly being called.

The Sister Sacred Sikkitili spouses come and descend.
All very cold very cold.
The spouses come descending.

Indeed they are in place in their abode they are watching over their
    abode. 230
They are really making their abode cool.

They are really learning about the patient.

pe wini sakki tirpa ulu arpatyekwici.
ipe nuselupillisekaye.

an inna ipekkwa yapakilakkwatina.   235
ka purpa ueletemalatti.
purpa uemaytemalatti.
ka purpati pali tampokena.
purpa pali tammipamakkekwanai.

an inna ipekkwa yapakilakkwati.   240
inna ipekkwa yapakila apalisa ueletemalatti.
apalis uemaytemalatti.
apalis pali tampokenai.
apalis pali tammipamakkekwanai.

an inna ipekkwa yapakilakkwakala.   245
mola ueletemalatti mola pali tampokenai.
mola pali tammipamakkekwanai.

an inna ipekkwa yapakilakkwakal.
apakan ueletemalatti.
apakan uemaytemalatti.   250
ka apakan pali tampokenai.
apakan pali tammipamakkekwanai.

an inna ipekkwa yapakilakkwakala.
ka kurkin ueletemalattiye.
kurkina   uemaytemalattiye.   255
ka kurkin pali tampokenai.
kurkin pali tammipamakkekwa.

an inna ipekkwa yapakilakkwakala.
sayliki ueletemalatti.
sayliki uemaytemalattiye.   260

sayliki pali tampokenai.
sayliki pali tammipamakkekwanaiye.

an inna ipekkwa yapakilakkwa.

inna iawala kialete.
inna war kiamaytemalattiye.   265

iawar pal ekaenai.
iawala pali tutturmakkekwanaiye.

Your tiny seeds are falling.
On top of the boulders.

Our owner of chicha's little one.   235
His soul has become very feverish.
His soul is very feverish.
Be cooling off his soul again for him.
Really making his soul cool again.

Our owner of chicha's little one.   240
The owner of chicha's little one's body fluid has become very feverish.
His body fluid is very feverish.
Be cooling off his body fluid again.
Really making his body fluid cool again.

Our owner of chicha's child.   245
His clothes have become very feverish be cooling off his clothes again.
Really making his clothes cool again.

Our owner of chicha's little one.
His body has become very feverish.
His body is very feverish.   250
Be cooling off his body again for him.
Really making his body cool again.

Our owner of chicha's little one.
His brain has become very feverish.
His brain   is very feverish.   255
Be cooling off his brain again for him.
Really making his brain cool again.

Our owner of chicha's little one.
His hair has become very feverish.
His hair is very feverish.   260

Be cooling off his hair again.
Really making his hair cool again.

Our owner of chicha's little one.

His chicha path has become clogged.
His chicha path is very clogged.   265

Be opening his path again.
Really making his path straight again.

an inna ipekkwayapakilakkwa.
tala itsotemalatti.
tala kakatemalatti.   270
ka tala pali tutturmakkenanai.
tala pali kannokenaiye.

nekati ainakkwaye neka paliye.
ti tukku tola walepunkanse sunna na okole.

puna inati pinwetili walepunkanse sunna okoleta.   275

tammipa tola walepunkan aitealiye.
pel apa tammipale tammipalepiye.

na kalupi kaenai kalu etarpenai.
kalu tammipamakkekwanai.
na pinakinet wisikuenaiye.   280

pe wini sakki tirpa ulu arpatyekwici.
ipe nuselupillisekaye.

pel apa tammipalepiye.

nekati ainakkwaye neka pali.
tammipa tola walepunkanse sunna okoletake.   285

puna inati ulupa nele.
walepunkanse sunna okoletake.

tammipa tola walepunkan aiteketake.
pel apa tammipalepiye.

na kalupi kaenai kalu etarpenai.   290
kalu tammipamakkekwanai.
na pinakinet wisikuenai.

nekati ainakkwaye neka pali.
tammipa tola walepunkanse sunna okoleta.

puna inati ututili walepunkan aiteketakeye.   295

Our owner of chicha's little one.
His vision has become very damaged.
His vision seems very misty.   270
Be making his vision straight again for him.
Strengthening his vision again for him.

At the place of the rising sun.
The River Source People spouses are indeed truly called.

The Sister Sacred Pinwetili (name of medicinal plant) spouses are truly
    called.   275

The Cooling Off People spouses begin to descend.
All very cold very cold.

Indeed they are in place in their abode they are watching over their
    abode.
They are really making their abode cool.
Indeed they are learning about the patient.   280

Your tiny seeds are falling.
On top of the boulders.

All very cold.

At the place of the rising sun.
The Cooling Off People spouses truly come and are called.   285

The Sister Sacred Urwa tree (name of medicine).
Spouses truly come and are called.

The Cooling Off People spouses come and descend.
All very cold.

Indeed they are in place in their abode they are watching over their
    abode.   290
They are really making their abode cool.
Indeed they are learning about the patient.

At the place of the rising sun.
The Cooling Off People spouses are truly called.

The Sister Sacred Ututili (name of small medicinal tree) spouses come
    and descend.   295

pel apa tammipale tammipalepiye.
walepunkan aiteketake.

na kalupi kaenai kalu etarpenai.
kalu tammipamakkekwanaiye.

pinakinet wisikuekwanaiye.   300

pe wini sakki tirpa ulu arpatyekwici.
ipe nuselupilliseye.

an inna ipekkwa yapakilakkwati purpa ueletemalattiye.
purpa uemaytemalatti.
ka purpati pali tampokenanaiye.   305
purpa pali tammipamakkekwanaiye.

an inna ipekkwa yapakilakkwatina.

apalisa ueletemalatti.
apalis uemaytemalattiye.

apalisa pali tampokenai.   310
apalis pali tammipamakkekwanaiye.

an inna ipekkwa yapakilakkwaka.
mola ueletemalatti.
mola uemaytemalatti.
molati pali tampokenai.   315
mola pali tammipamakkekwanai.

an inna ipekkwa yapakilakkwati.
apakan ueletemalatti.
apakan ueletetiye.

apakan pali tampokenanai.   320
apakan pali tammipamakkekwanaiye.

an inna ipekkwa yapakilakkwakala.
kurkin ueletemalatti.
kurkin uemaytemalattiye.
ka kurkina pali tampokenai.   325
kurkin pali tammipamakkekwanaiye.

All very cold very cold.
The spouses come and descend.

Indeed they are in place in their abode they are watching over their
    abode.
They are really making their abode cool.

They are really learning about the patient.   300

Your tiny seeds are falling.
On top of the boulders.

Our owner of chicha's little one's soul has become very feverish.
His soul is very feverish.
Be cooling off his soul again for him.   305
Really making his soul cool again.

And our owner of chicha's little one.

His body fluid has become very feverish.
His body fluid is very feverish.

Be cooling off his body fluid again.   310
Really making his body fluid cool again.

Our owner of chicha's little one.
His clothes have become very feverish.
His clothes are very feverish.
Be cooling off his clothes again.   315
Really making his clothes cool again.

Our owner of chicha's little one.
His body has become very feverish.
His body has become feverish.

Be cooling off his body again.   320
Really making his body cool again.

Our owner of chicha's little one.
His brain has become very feverish.
His brain is very feverish.
Be cooling off his brain again for him.   325
Really making his head cool again.

an inna ipekkwa yapakilakkwakala.
sayliki ueletemalatti.
sayliki uemaytema.

ka sayliki pali tampokenai.   330
sayliki pali tammipamakkekwa.

an inna ipekkwa yapakilakkwakala.
inna iawala kialeteti.
iawar kiamaytemalattiye.
ka iawar pal ekaenai.   335
iawar pali tutturmakkekwanaiye.

an inna ipekkwa yapakilakkwakala.
tala itsotemalatti.
tala tar kakatemalattiye.
tala pali kannokenai.   340
tala pali tutturmakkekwanai.

nekati ainakkwaye neka pali.
tammipa tola walepunkanse sunna na okolemekwiye.

puna inati urwatili walepunkan aiteketake.
pel apa tammipalepiye.   345

tarpapilli pe mola sailakan akikinnekwici.
tarpapilli pe mola sailakan uurmakkekwiciye.

pel apa tammipale tammipalepiye.

nekati ainakkwaye neka paliye.

tammipa tola walepunkanse sunna okolemaiye.   350

puna inati urwatili walepunkan aiteketake pel apa tammipalepiye.

tammipa tola walepunkan aitekenaiye.

tarpapilli pe mola sailakan akikinnekwiciye.
tarpapilli   pe mola sailakan uurmakkekwiciye.

pel apa tammipalepiye.   355

an inna ipekkwa yapakilakkwa.

Our owner of chicha's little one.
His hair has become very feverish.
His hair is very feverish.

Be cooling off his hair again for him.   330
Really making his hair cool again.

Our owner of chicha's little one.
His chicha path has become clogged.
His path is very clogged.
Be opening his path again for him.   335
Really making his path straight again.

Our owner of chicha's little one.
His vision has become very damaged.
His vision seems very misty.
Be strengthening his vision again.   340
Really making his vision straight again.

At the place of the rising sun.
The Cooling Off People spouses are indeed truly being called.

The Sister Sacred Urwatili (name of medicinal plant that grows near
    lakes and the mouths of rivers) spouses come and descend.
All very cold.   345

In the breeze your clothes (leaves) are standing rustling.
In the breeze your clothes are standing sounding.

All very cold very cold.

At the place of the rising sun.

The Cooling Off People spouses are truly being called.   350

The Sister Sacred Urwatili spouses come and descend all very cold.

The Cooling Off People spouses are descending.

In the breeze your clothes are standing rustling.
In the breeze   your clothes are standing sounding.

All very cold.   355

Our owner of chicha's little one.

ka purpa ueletemalatti.
purpa uemaytemala.

ka purpati pali tampokenai.
purpa pali tammipamakkekwa.   360

an inna ipekkwa yapakilakkwakala.
apalisa ueletemalatti.
apalisa uemaytemalatti.

apalis pali tampokenaiye.
apalis pali tammipamakkekwanaiye.   365

an inna ipekkwa yapakilakkwakala.

ka mola ueletemalatti.
ka mola uemaytemalattiye.

ka molati pali tampokenai.
mola pali tammipamakkekwanaiye.   370

an inna ipekkwa yapakilakkwa.

apakan ueletemalatti.
apakan uemayte.

ka apakan pali tampokenanai.
apakana pali tammipamakkekwanaiye.   375

an inna ipekkwa yapakilakkwaka.
ka kurkina ueletemalatti.
kurkin uemaytemalaye.
ka kurkina pali tampokenai.
kurkin pali tammipamakkekwanaiye.   380

an inna ipekkwa yapakilakkwakala.
sayliki ueletemalatti.
sayliki uemaytemala.
ka sayliki pali tampokenai.
sayliki pali tammipamakkekwanai.   385

an inna ipekkwa yapakilakkwaka.
inna iawala kialete.
iawar kiamaytemalattiye.

His soul has become very feverish.
His soul is very feverish.

Be cooling off his soul again for him.
Really making his soul cool again.   360

Our owner of chicha's little one.
His body fluid has become very feverish.
His body fluid is very feverish.

Be cooling off his body fluid again.
Really making his body fluid cool again.   365

Our owner of chicha's little one.

His clothes have become very feverish.
His clothes are very feverish.

Be cooling off his clothes again for him.
Really making his clothes cool again.   370

Our owner of chicha's little one.

His body has become very feverish.
His body is feverish.

Be cooling off his body again for him.
Really making his body cool again.   375

Our owner of chicha's little one.
His brain has become very feverish.
His brain is very feverish.
Be cooling off his brain again for him.
Really making his brain cool again.   380

Our owner of chicha's little one.
His hair has become very feverish.
His hair is very feverish.
Be cooling off his hair again for him.
Really making his hair cool again.   385

Our owner of chicha's little one.
His chicha path has become clogged.
His path is very clogged.

ka iawar pal ekaenai.
iawar pali tutturmakkekwanaiye.   390

an inna ipekkwa yapakilakkwaka.

ka tala itsotemalatti.
tala kakatemalattiye.

tala pali kannokenai.
tala pali tutturmakkekwanaiye.   395

nekati ainakkwaye neka pali.
tammipa tola walepunkanse sunna okoleye.

puna inati appatili walepunkanse sunna okoleta.

tammipa tola walepunkan aiteketake.
pel apa tammipalepiye.   400

tammipa tola walepunkan aiteketa.

pe wini sakki tirpa ulu arpatyekwici.
ipe nuselupilliseye.

nekati ainakkwa neka pali.
tammipa tola walepunkanse sunna okoleta.   405

puna inati appatili walepunkan aitealiye.
pel apa tammipale tammipalepi.

walepunkan aiteketake.

na kalupi kaenai kalu etarpenai.
kalu tammipamakkekwanaiye.   410

pinakinet wisikuekwanaiye.

pe wini sakki tirpa ulu arpatyekwici.
ipe nuselupillisekaye.

Be opening his path again for him.
Really making his path straight again. 390

Our owner of chicha's little one.

His vision has become very damaged.
His vision seems very misty.

Be strengthening his vision again.
Really making his vision straight again. 395

At the place of the rising sun.
The Cooling Off People spouses are truly called.

The Sister Sacred Appatili (name of a medicinal plant that grows on the
banks of rivers and has fragrant smelling flowers) spouses are truly
called.

The Cooling Off People spouses come and descend.
All very cold. 400

The Cooling Off People spouses come and descend.

Your tiny seeds are falling.
On top of the boulders.

At the place of the rising sun.
The Cooling Off People spouses are truly called. 405

The Sister Sacred Appatili spouses begin to descend.
All very cold very cold.

The spouses come and descend.

Indeed they are in place in their abode they are watching over their
abode.
They are really making their abode cool. 410

They are really learning about the patient.

Your tiny seeds are falling.
On top of the boulders.

an inna ipekkwa yapakilakkwaka.
purpa ueletemalatti.   415
ka purpa uemaytemalatti.
ka purpati pali tampokenanai.
purpa pali tammipamakkekwanaiye.

an inna ipekkwa yapakilakkwakala.
apalisa ueleteye.   420
apalis uemaytemalatti.
ka apalis pali tampokenai.
apalis pali tammipamakkekwanaiye.

an inna ipekkwa yapakilakkwakalaye.
ka mola ueletemalatti.   425
mola uemaytemalattiye.
ka molati pali tampokenai.
mola pali tammipamakkekwanai.

an inna ipekkwa yapakilakkwakala.
apakan ueletemalatti.   430
apakan uemaytemalattiye.

apakan pali tampokenaiye.
apaken pali tammipamakkekwanaiye.

an inna ipekkwa yapakilakkwakala.
kurkin ueletemalatti.   435
kurkin uemaytema.
ka kurkina pali tampokenai.
kurkin pali tammipamakkekwanaiye.

an inna ipekkwa yapakilakkwakala.
saylikia ueletemalatti.   440
sayliki ueletema.
sayliki pali tampokenai.
sayliki pali tammipamakke.

an inna ipekkwa yapakilakkwa.
inna iawala kialeteti.   445
inna iawar kiamaytemalat.
ka iawar pal ekaenai.
iawar pali tutturmakkekwanaiye.

an inna ipekkwa yapakila.
tala itsotemalatti.   450

Our owner of chicha's little one.
His soul has become very feverish.   415
His soul is very feverish.
Be cooling off his soul again for him.
Really making his soul cool again.

Our owner of chicha's little one.
His body fluid has become feverish.   420
His body fluid is very feverish.
Be cooling off his body fluid again for him.
Really making his body fluid cool again.

Our owner of chicha's little one.
His clothes have become very feverish.   425
His clothes are very feverish.
Be cooling off his clothes again for him.
Really making his clothes cool again.

Our owner of chicha's child.
His body has become very feverish.   430
His body is very feverish.

Be cooling off his body again.
Really making his body cool again.

Our owner of chicha's little one.
His brain has become very feverish.   435
His brain is very feverish.
Be cooling off his brain again for him.
Really making his brain cool again.

Our owner of chicha's little one.
His hair has become very feverish.   440
His hair has become quite feverish.
Be cooling off his hair again.
Making his hair cool again.

Our owner of chicha's little one.
His chicha path has become clogged.   445
His chicha path is very clogged.
Be opening his path again for him.
Really making his path straight again.

Our owner of chicha's little one.
His vision has become very damaged.   450

tala tar kakaketemala.
ka tala pali kannokenana.
tala pali tutturmakkekwana.

nelekan tarpa oimakkenai kanakwa tarpa oimakkeyolakiye.
pela tammipa tola walepunkana otimaysatakketikineye.   455

pela tammipa tola walepunkana otimaysatakketikine.
nelekan tarpa oimakkekwayolakiye.

pela naikwatil ukakkase.
pel akkusakwal ukakkase.
pela tammipa tola walepunkana urpisa.   460
apisua tar takketikine.

an inna ipekkwa yapakilakkwatina.
ipe kala kunpakkekwatise.
peki apalluytokuye.
nelekan tal uanaemala.   465
pepi sunna tar wisimoiniye.
nelekana na tar pe uanae.

His vision seems very misty.
Be strengthening his vision again for him.
Really making his vision straight again.

The spirits are calling out the specialist is also calling out.
Now that all the Cooling Off People spouses have gathered.   455

Now that all the Cooling Off People spouses have gathered.
The spirits are also calling out.

Up to every part of them.
Up to the last part of them.
All of the Cooling Off People spouses are in place.   460
Now that they have come to the specialist.

And our owner of chicha's little one.
After four days and nights.
He will be bathed with you (the plants whose spirits have been
    counseled).
The spirits are all counseled.   465
You who truly know.
Spirits you are indeed counseled.

Photo 1. Pedro Arias speaking in the Mulatuppu gathering house

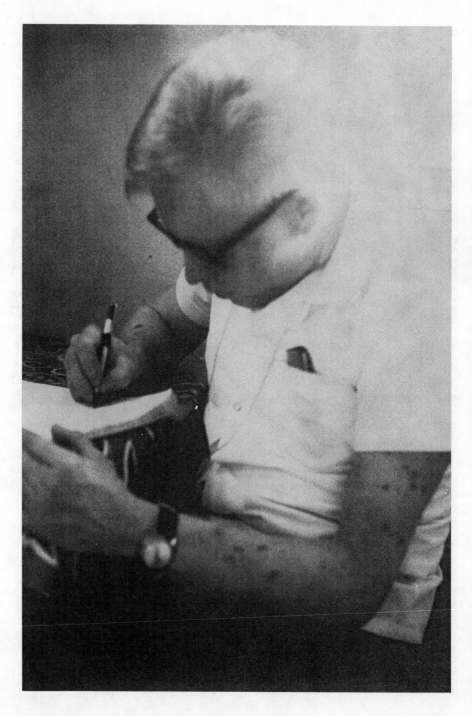

Photo 2. *Hortenciano Martínez writing in a notebook*

Photo 3. Chief Nipakkinya watching a sporting event

Photo 4. Anselmo Urrutia working with a tape recorder

Photo 5. *Pranki Pilos wearing his medicinal specialist's clothing and carrying his staff*

Photo 6. *Olowiktinappi gathering medicine in the jungle*

Photo 7. *(above)*
Olowiktinappi making a basket

Photo 8. *(left) Olowiktinappi
performing* The Way of the
Rattlesnake

Photo 9. *Chief Mastaletat*

Photo 10. Woman grinding sugarcane to make chicha

Photo 11. Men grinding sugarcane to make chicha

Photo 12. Chicha in pots

Photo 13. *(above) Men stirring chicha*

Photo 14. *(right) Chicha fermenting*

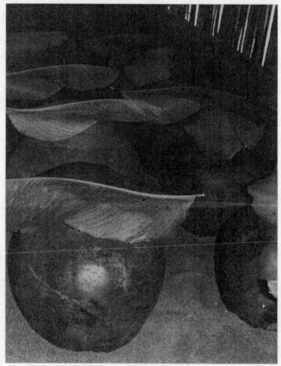

Photo 15. *Pedro Arias sitting in front of fermented chicha*

Photo 16. *Kantule Ernesto Linares and his assistant, Andrew García, performing during puberty rites*

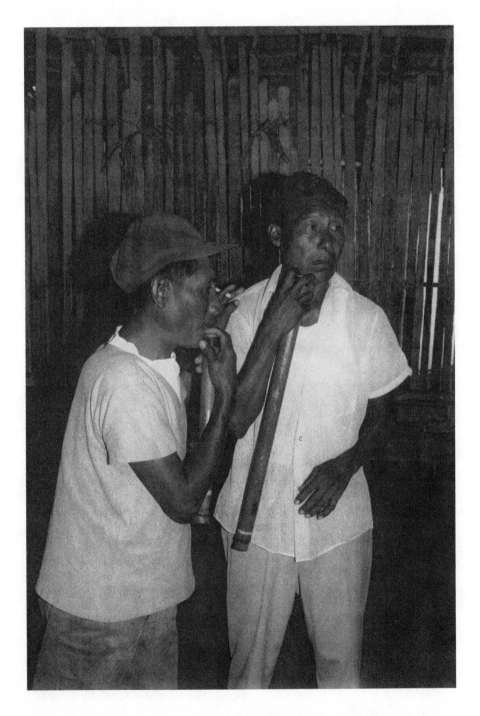

Photo 17. Meristante Díaz and Rogelio Robles playing long flutes during puberty festivities

Photo 18. *Women preparing ritual meal for puberty festivities*

Photo 19. *Women eating ritual meal during puberty festivities*

Photo 20. Men eating ritual meal during puberty festivities

Photo 21. *Jerónimo Green and Alfredo Martínez preparing hammock for puberty festivities*

Photo 22. *The island/village of Mulatuppu*

Photo 23. *Tiowilikinya*

Photo 24. *Juliana Quijano dressed for puberty festivities*

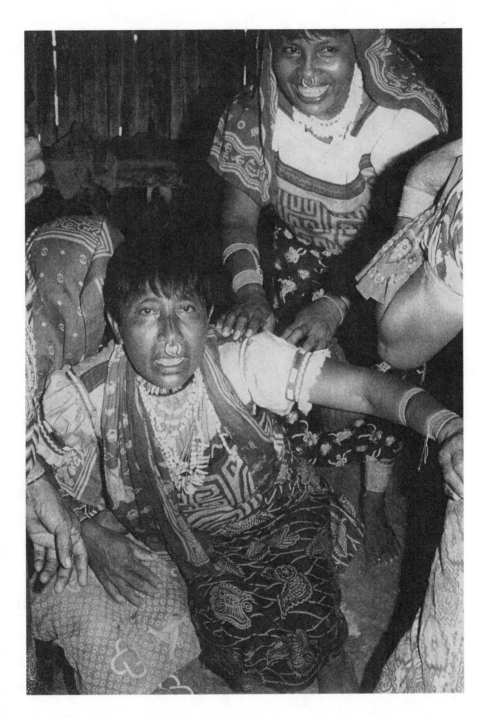

Photo 25. *Women at puberty festivities*

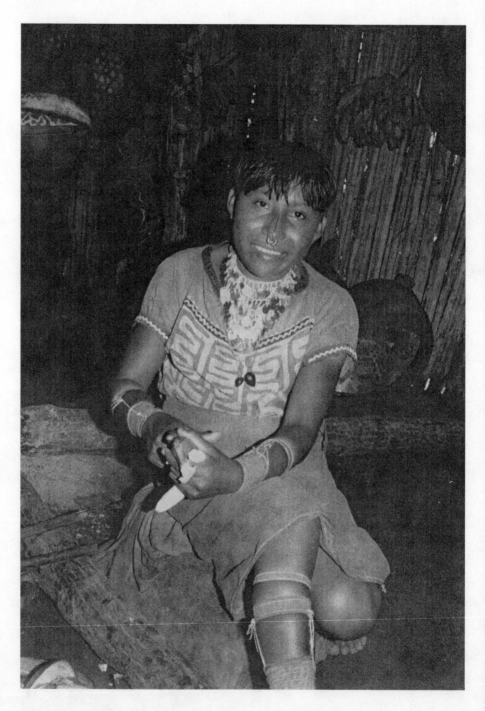

Photo 26. *Woman at puberty festivities*

Photo 27. *Women at puberty festivities*

Photo 28. Benilda Quijano with baby

Figure 14. Hunting a dangerous snake

Chapter 8

The Way of the Rattlesnake

Performed by Olowiktinappi

Ukkunaipe ikar/The Way of the Rattlesnake was performed by Olowiktinappi in a home in Mulatuppu on March 13, 1970. *The Way of the Rattlesnake* is a genre of Kuna literature that is oriented to magical and curing practices. It is a member of a large but endangered set of chants that are addressed to representatives of the spirit world and are in their ritual, esoteric language (as are several of the other chants represented in this book). *The Way of the Rattlesnake* is performed to the spirit of a snake that the Kuna consider to be a good snake, the rattlesnake, in order to protect against bites and attacks by the many other evil and dangerous snakes and snake spirits that are found in the Kuna jungle environment.

Olowiktinappi, who died in 1975 at the age of seventy-three, was a renowned Kuna political leader and ritual specialist. He was an *arkar* "chief's spokesman" in the village of Mulatuppu and knowledgeable of the myths, legends, and history of the Kuna. He was quiet and soft spoken, but a strong intellect and hard-working man, with a marvelous and subtle sense of humor. He was best known for his knowledge of curing and medicine—he knew well the medicinal properties of plants in the jungle and gathered them for family members and patients. He also knew many curing chants, among them *The Way of the Hat,* for curing headaches and *The Way of the Hot Pepper,* for curing high fever. He also knew chants for acquiring abilities, such as *The Way of the Basil Plant,* used for successful hunting, and chants for protection against disease and misfortune, such as *The Way of the Rattlesnake.* In 1970 the village of Mulatuppu sent Olowiktinappi, with a scholarship, to a village in the Darien jungle to study traditional snakebite medicine and associated chants, because he was already knowledgeable in this area.[1]

What is represented here is the opening episode of *The Way of the Rattlesnake*. It is part of a much longer chant, which unfortunately I never recorded. I include it in this book both because of its poetic qualities and because, as far as I know, it is now extinct. This is surely the only recorded version of it in existence.

The Way of the Rattlesnake protects its knower and performer, as well as others for whom it is performed, from dangerous snakes and snake spirits, by using Rattlesnake as a helper. The chant describes how Rattlesnake hunts other snakes in order to provide food for his wife, and thereby protects humans from these dangerous snakes.

Like other curing and magical chants *The Way of the Rattlesnake* is reflexive and metacommunicative. It opens with a description of the specialist/knower (a spirit version of Olowiktinappi) in his hammock calling to Rattlesnake, using Rattlesnake's secret spirit name, Sacred Ukkupana Sure Shot Man. From under the hammock rises the smoke of chicha, cocoa, and tobacco, which have magical, medicinal properties. Again as in other curing and magical chants, the knower demonstrates his knowledge of the spirit to be controlled, in this case the Rattlesnake spirit, by stating that he knows his origins and foundations. The narrative of the chant then begins. It consists of a series of episodes, which describe in the spirit world what the performer Olowiktinappi wants to happen in the real world and which actually do happen, as the chant is performed. Rattlesnake calls his wife, in her secret spirit name, Sister Sacred Kunipyaisop, who helps him prepare himself to leave home and go to battle with evil spirits, those of dangerous snakes. Sister Sacred Kunipyaisop is called his primary spouse. Apparently Kuna spirits have more than one wife, as quite possibly real Kuna used to. Rattlesnake describes the battle he expects to have and how he will fight. There is a long and very poetic description of Rattlesnake's home as he leaves it and of the medicines he will employ.

The spirit world portrayed in *The Way of the Rattlesnake*, in an esoteric, ritual language, is a mirror image, from the Kuna point of view, of everyday Kuna life. The chant describes in slow-moving detail such activities as cooking on a fire, preparing oneself for a trip, and drinking a beverage. Lines and sets of lines are repeated with slight variations, creating the parallelistic patterns characteristic of Kuna curing and magical performances and resulting in a slow moving narration describing objects, actions, activities, and movements in gradually evolving perspectives. Through these lines one can imagine a Kuna woman, early in the morning, preparing *chukula*, the banana-based beverage Kuna drink before beginning a day of work.

She is preparing the ritual fire.
She is stirring the ritual fire.
On top of the ritual fire.
The ritual flames are sparkling.
The ritual flames are rising.
On top of the ritual fire.
She is placing the ritual cooking pot.
Inside the ritual cooking pot.
She was sitting placing the ritual beverage's fruit (ripe banana)
    she was.
She was sitting pouring the ritual beverage she was.
The ritual beverage is bubbling.
The ritual beverage is boiling.
The ritual beverage is boiling and boiling.
Sacred Ukkupana Sure Shot Man, is standing twirling himself
    about.
He is standing moving himself back and forth within his abode.

Conversations between husband and wife are quoted directly, as is characteristic of all forms of Kuna speaking and chanting. This seemingly banal verbal exchange is a typical Kuna conversational routine, including explicit discussion of the day's activities.

Sister Sacred Kunipyaisop is addressing him.
"You will go and get aliment (food) for me, you will go and
    pursue aliment for me" she says she does.
"I will prepare a beverage for you."
Sacred Ukkupana's spouse (says).

GRAMMAR, STYLE, AND VOCABULARY

The Way of the Rattlesnake contains certain grammatical features characteristic of Kuna magical and curing chants. Many words, especially line-final words, end in the optative/subjunctive suffix *ye*, which both serves as a poetic line-final marker and conveys a mystical, optative tone to the chant. Morphemes typically occur in their long form, containing the final vowel that is usually deleted in everyday speech. There is an extensive use of suffixes of body position, which are crucial to the magical efficacy of the chant in that they are part of the detailed description of activities essential to magical power. Certain grammatical affixes and combinations of affixes are unique to this genre.

Many words in *The Way of the Rattlesnake* are different from the words used to label the same object or activity in everyday Kuna; they are esoteric, metaphorical, and playful. Here are some examples:

Everyday Kuna	Way of the Rattlesnake	English
neka	*posumpa*	house
ome	*walepunkwa*	wife
kopet	*ipe mimiryo*	drink
tule	*inna ipet* (owner of chicha)	person
masi	*kirpala*	food
kope	*puylusae*	to drink
ipya	*tala*	eyes
ope	*yatwe*	to get washed

In order to render the Kuna feel and mood in this text, I have translated *posumpa* as abode, *walepunkwa* as spouse, *ipe mimiryo* as sacred beverage, *kirpala* as aliment, *puylusae* as imbibe, *tala* as vision, and *yatwe* as bathe. I have translated *inna ipet* literally, as owner of chicha.

The use of an elaborate and esoteric vocabulary and great attention to descriptions of movements and motions, lights and flames, sounds and atmospheric conditions, protecting and watching over, and killing and being killed enable the creation of a highly poetic text.

> Sacred Ukkupana Sure Shot Man goes and steps himself forward.
> He goes and drifts himself away, he goes and speeds himself along quickly.
> Along the path of obtaining aliment.
> Along the path of animal aliment.
>
> And Sacred Ukkupana's principal portals.
> Are standing sounding the different tones cannot be distinguished.
> All like *kalili* bugs.
> The principal portals are standing sounding.
> All like *pilu pilu* bugs the principal portals are standing sounding.
> All in different ways, in different ways.
> The principal portals are standing sounding.

All like golden clocks.
Like golden baby clocks (pocket watches).
Sacred Ukkupana's principal portals are standing sounding.
The different tones cannot be distinguished.
The principal portals are standing chiming.
All like bells, like tiny bells.

All like accordions the principal entrances are standing
    sounding.
All differently all differently.
The principal entrances are standing sounding.
All like sacred thunder.
The principal portals are standing roaring.
The different tones could not be distinguished.

The tiny *napkiar* (medicinal plant) vines are going along
    climbing up.
Frightened frightened (by the taste) all bitter bitter.
All like dripping rain the stronghold is is misty.
Going along watching taking care of the stronghold.
The sacred medicines are going along climbing up.
All changing form changing form (appearing and disappearing)
    the sacred medicines are going along climbing up.

If with the enemy people's ritual rifle.
They flame (shoot) at my body at mine, at my skin mine say.
If they transform my skin into a sieve (shoot me full of holes)
    say.
If they extinguish my vision (eyes) (= kill me) you see say.

This chant depicts an imaginary world, far from everyday Kuna life,
but present in Kuna spirit life, a dynamic world of golden clocks and
pocket watches, bells and accordions, and doors that chime all kinds of
tones, bristling with activity, sound, and light. Because of its grammatical, lexical, and poetic features, *The Way of the Rattlesnake*, as all of the
texts in this book, poses fascinating challenges for translation.

Olokwagdi de Akwanusadup's beautiful and complex illustration for
this chant (fig. 14), "Hunting a Dangerous Snake," can be viewed in two
perspectives, by turning it upside down. The illustration represents Rattlesnake hunting a snake in two ways, one with a bow and arrow, the other
with a blowgun. Rattlesnake is shown in his human/spirit form, as a tra-

ditional Kuna hunter, with long hair and earrings. The fearful snake, fangs pointing outward, is the centerpiece of the illustration. My photographs show Olowiktinappi making a basket for carrying medicine, gathering medicine in the jungle, and performing *The Way of the Rattlesnake* (photos 6–8).

Here is *The Way of the Rattlesnake*, as performed by Olowiktinappi.

Figure 15. *Kuna man competes at drinking chicha with his wife*

Kuna

waiye.
apisuatinaye, pese purkala palimakkiteye.
apisuati pese purkala palimaye maikusaye.
neka pilli nerkwasekaye.
apisuati pese purkala suoekwamaiye.
"pe purpa nelekanti wisikus" sokekua "pe sailakan wisikus" sokekuye. 5
"apisuati pe purpa nelekan aitesatti wisikus" soke kuaye.
apisuatinaye e posumpa manaylali pillikine.
apisuati ipe pokachi pilli yalakwaleye.
pese purkalati palimakkite kuye.
apisuati inna tula apalakineye.   10
inna tonaka inna kelikkwa waka sipu tula apalakine.
apisuati pese purkala palimayekwa maikusaye.
nele kelilikkwa nele alulu tula nua apalakine.
apisuati pese purkalati suoekwamaiye.
inna tonaka inna toli toli waka sipu tula apalakine.   15
apisua pese tar kolekwamaikusaye.
inna tonaka inna toli toli alulu tula apalakine.
apisua pe nik kolemai, pe nuka saekwamaiye.
neka pilli nerkwakineye.
kalu sailakwa akkarpiye, apisu pe nik kolemaiye.   20
kalu tokia pilli akkarpiye.
apisua pese purkala palimaye maiye.
mani tokia pilli akkarpiye, apisu pese purkala palimakkiteye.
nele ukkupana kinki tule neka tar sun ittomai pela pokitikkikwaleye.
pela yakkiritikkikwaleye.   25
nele ukkupanaye.
kinki tule nekati tar sun ittomaiye.
"kanati pan nik kolemai, kana pani nuka saekwamaikusaye."
e posumpa manaklali tar pillikineye.
nele ukkupana kinki tule walepunse kolekwichikusaye.   30
nele ukkupana walepun sailatinaye, puna ina kunipyaisopse
    kolekwichiye.
maniti kunipyaisopse kolekwakwichi kusaye.
"na peka kirpar ononaeye na peka kirpala nikka ilekuenaemalaye.
kanati ani nuka saemai, ani nuka pipiemaiye."

English

waiye.
The specialist, addresses you.
The specialist was lying addressing you he was.
From the sixth level underground.
The specialist is lying chanting to you.
"He already knows your sacred soul" he says "he already knows your
    foundations" he says.   5
"The specialist already knows the landing (origin = birth) of your sacred
    soul" he says he does.
The specialist is on the upper level of his abode.
The specialist is lying in his ritual hammock.
The specialist addresses you he does.
The specialist is in the middle of live chicha.   10
In the middle of ceremonial chicha smoke and live pale (white) cocoa.
The specialist was lying addressing you he was.
In the very middle of sacred live pink cocoa.
The specialist is lying chanting to you.
In the middle of ceremonial *toli toli* chicha smoke and pale live
    tobacco.   15
The specialist was lying calling to you he was.
In the middle of ceremonial *toli toli* chicha smoke and live pink tobacco.
The specialist is lying calling directly to you, he is lying naming you.
In the sixth level underground.
At your strange foundational stronghold, the specialist is lying calling
    directly to you.   20
At the strange Tokia (name of place) stronghold level.
The specialist is lying addressing you.
At the strange silver Tokia stronghold level, the specialist addresses you.
Sacred Ukkupana (Rattlesnake's name) Sure Shot Man truly lies feeling
    all tranquil.
All silent.   25
Sacred Ukkupana
Sure Shot Man truly lies feeling in his house.
"You knower are lying calling directly to me, the knower was lying
    naming me he was."
On the upper level of his abode.
Sacred Ukkupana Sure Shot Man was standing calling his spouse
    he was.   30
And sacred Ukkupana is standing calling his primary spouse, Sister
    Sacred Kunipyaisop (her name).
He was standing calling Sister Sacred Kunipyaisop he was.
"I will go and get aliment (consisting of other snakes) for you I will go
    and pursue an animal for you.
The knower is lying naming me, he is lying calling out my name."

kana e posumpa tikkalapaliye.   35
kirpalati neka ipekute ete na takkeye.
"teeti eka nikka ilekuepi tar 'pani sunna peti unaleye.'
kana pan nik kolemaikusaye."
puna ina kunipyaisop palimakkialiye.
"panka kirpal ononaeye, panka kirpala nikka ilekuenae" soke kuye.   40
"na peka ipe mimiryote ulu takkoiniye."
nele ukkupana walepunkwatinaye, ipe alulukina takkaliye.
ipe alulu ul omukkualiye.
ipe alulu aklakineye.
ipe alulukana kunamakkaliye.   45
ipe alulukan kwapunnualiye.
ipe alulu aklakkineye.
ipe koalikampi ulu tar sialiye.
ipe koaliye yaakineye.
ipe mimiryo winikampi urpesiikwisaye.   50
ipe mimiryopi ulu opatyesikwisaye.
ipe mimiryokanapa mummusmaaliye.
ipe mimiryokanapa mumuryamakkaliye.
ipe mimiryokanapa kwakwasmakkaliye.
nele ukkupana kinki tuleye, pupa wal aypiryekwakwichiye.   55
pupa wal muchuppimakkekwakwichi e posumpa nekakineye.
e posumpa ukakka paliye, ipe iititi walakan ainakkwekwakwichiye.
ipe iititi pilli yalapa pupa nakkwenaye.
man aklali pillisekaye.
man aklali pilli ukakkapaliye.   60
pupa wal ituamakkena pupa muchuppimakkenae.
ye olo putipi tar kaekwichi kusaye.
nele ukkupana kinki tuletinaye.
ipeye napakiwal ulu tar kaekwakwichi kusaye.
olo sikupi tar kaekwichikusaye.   65
ye pila tola tintuli totokkwapi tar kaekwichikusaye.
kirpalate ilekute sokeleye.
kirpala ittimiekala, kirpar koamakkekalaye.
olo puti opiryekwichi neka ainakkwa sikkiye.
olo siku opiryekwakwichi neka ainakkwa sikkiye.   70
olo sikuka pup aipiryetakeye.
olo sikuka pup aipilialiye.
ipe ititi pillise pup aiteketakeye.
ipe upikka pillise pup aitekekwichikusaye.
kana pilli ailakki olo puti opiryetakeye.   75

Around the abode of the knower.   35
The aliment dwells at home it seems.
"He wants me to pursue an animal for him 'you for me truly you
    therefore.'
You knower were lying calling directly to me you were."
Sister Sacred Kunipyaisop is addressing him.
"You will go and get aliment for me, you will go and pursue aliment
    for me" she says she does.   40
"I will prepare a beverage for you."
Sacred Ukkupana's spouse (says), she is preparing the ritual fire.
She is stirring the ritual fire.
On top of the ritual fire.
The ritual flames are sparkling.   45
The ritual flames are rising.
On top of the ritual fire.
She is placing the ritual cooking pot.
Inside the ritual cooking pot.
She was sitting placing the ritual beverage's fruit (ripe banana) she
    was.   50
She was sitting pouring the ritual beverage she was.
The ritual beverage is bubbling.
The ritual beverage is boiling.
The ritual beverage is boiling and boiling.
Sacred Ukkupana Sure Shot Man, is standing twirling himself about. 55
He is standing moving himself back and forth within his abode.
Beside his abode, the ritual ladders are standing rising up.
He goes and climbs himself up the ritual ladder.
To the upper level.
Up to the upper level.   60
He goes and steps himself forward he goes and moves himself back
    and forth.
He was standing holding his very golden blowgun he was.
And Sacred Ukkupana Sure Shot Man.
He was standing holding his ritual bow he was.
He was standing holding his very golden arrow he was.   65
He was standing holding his tiny enemy's knife he was.
When he pursues aliment say.
In order to apportion aliment, in order to cut the aliment into pieces.
He is standing signalling the golden blowgun to where the sun rises.
He is standing signalling the golden arrow to where the sun rises. 70
He comes and twirls himself about with the golden arrow.
He is twirling himself about with the golden arrow.
He comes and descends himself down the golden ladder.
He was standing landing himself to the ritual earth he was.
He comes and signals the golden blowgun over the knower on the
    upper level.   75

kana pilli ailakki olo siku opiryekwakwichiye.
walepunkwase pup aipiryekwichi ulu sumpa totokkwa nekasekaye.
"na peka ipe mimiryo ulu tar okuteiniye."
walepun saila tar palimaye sikwisaye.
"panka kirpar ononae panka kirpala nikka ilekuenae" tar soke kuye. 80
ipe mimiryoki puklusaaliye.
nele ukkupana kinki tuleti.
ipe mimiryoki puklu wal alimakkesiye.
nele ukkupana kinki tuletinaye.
ipe mimiryo ulu sapoaliye, olo supa we na tarpaliye. 85
ipe mimiryo ulu otoaliye.
"kirpala nikka ilekute" sokeleye.
"na kirpalapa penekutema" sokeleye.
"naki puklusaekalaye.
naki pukluye. 90
saekwichi kuekalaye."
ipe waikwapi ulu otokwichi olo supa we na tarpaliye.
nele ukkupana kinki tuletinaye.
tula nelekampi ulu sapoaliye.
olo supa we na tarpaliye. 95
tula nelekanki na onoekalaye.
tula nelekanki pupa wala yatwekalaye.
"kirpalati tule kinki tule" sokemoiniye.
"ani olo supa we na tarpaliye.
man ansuelu ulu tar pioyte" sokeleye. 100
"tula nelekanki pupa wala yatwekalaye.
tula nelekanki onoekalaye."
tula nelekampi sapokwichi olo supa we na tarpaliye.
nele ukkupana kinki tuleye.
walepunkwaka sunnamaaliye. 105
"kanaka posumpate etarpenaemalaye.
kana alisokenaemalaye.
kana irwa nakkulekekwanaeye.
inna ipekanka neka pilli penetakkenae.
inna ipekanka neka pilli tampoenaemaliniye." 110
nele ukkupan walepunse nappi kolekwichiye.
"inna ipekan irwalaye.
neka pilli okoppenaemalaye.
inna ipekan itualeye.
neka pilli penetakkenaemaliniye." 115

nele ukkupana kinki tule, walepun saila sunnamaliye.
"ipe kala kwinpikwa pani oeto summaye?"
nele ukkupan walepun nappi tar kolekwichiye.
"ipe kala kunpakkekwa na peki pupa walakante oweletoiniye.

He is standing signalling the golden arrow over the knower on the upper
    level.
He is standing twirling himself toward his spouse toward the tiny hearth.
"The ritual beverage is ready for you."
The primary spouse was sitting addressing (him) she was.
"You will go and get aliment for me you will go and pursue aliment for
    me" she says she does.   80
He is imbibing his ritual beverage.
Sacred Ukkupana Sure Shot Man.
He is sitting filling his gourd with the beverage.
And Sacred Ukkupana Sure Shot Man.
He is covering his ritual beverage, inside his golden coat.   85
He is hiding his ritual drink.
"When I pursue aliment" he says.
"When I compete with aliment" he says.
"In order to imbibe.
To imbibe.   90
In order to be standing doing this."
He is standing hiding his ritual cord inside his golden coat.
And Sacred Ukkupana Sure Shot Man.
He is covering his live sacred medicines.
Inside his golden coat.   95
In order to protect himself with live sacred medicines.
In order to bathe himself with live sacred medicines.
"The aliment man (other snakes) is a sure shot man" he says.
"If by chance inside my golden coat.
He nails his silver hooks (fangs)" he says.   100
"In order to bathe myself with live sacred medicines.
In order to protect myself with live sacred medicines."
He is standing covering live sacred medicines inside his golden coat.
Sacred Ukkupana Sure Shot Man.
He is speaking to his spouse.   105
"We will go and take care of the abode of the knower.
We will go and alleviate the knower.
We will go and guard in front of the knower.
We will go and help the owners of chicha (people) all over the earth.
Let us go and cool off the owners of chicha all over the earth."   110
Sacred Ukkupana is standing calling to his spouse one more time.
"In front of the owners of chicha.
To calm all over the earth.
Before the owners of chicha.
Let us go and help all over the earth."   115

Sacred Ukkupana Sure Shot Man's, primary spouse is speaking.
"For how many days will you be lost from me?"
Sacred Ukkupana's spouse is standing calling one more time.
"I will disappear myself from you for four days.

ipe kala kunpakkekwa na peki pupa walakante owelete pe takkeleye. 120
pupa wala kante wialete pe takke sokele.
inna ipekana posumpa sokakwen sikkimalattiye.
ani kana penekutemalattiye.
ete nui an epinsappitoe kep ipi sokekwaye."
nele ukkupan tar palimakkialiye.   125
"inna ipekana ani kana penekutemalattiye
pila tola ipe kupettu walakankineye.
ani ulukkate aniye, pupawalate anki kwapunnute sokekwaleye.
ani ulukkakante pukpumayte sokekwaleye.
ani tala okitte pe takke sokekwaleye.   130
ipe kala kunpakkekwa na peki pupa walakante oweletoiniye."
walepunkwase nappi kolekwichiye.
"inna ipekante ani ulukkakante ealite pe takkeleye.
inna ipekante kepe nui epinsatemo" ipi sokekwaye.
"neka pilli nerkwaki kalikia, totokkwa ipekankalaye.   135
na ulamakkenae semoiniye."
nele ukkupan walepunse nappi kolekwichiye.
nele ukkupana kinkin tule pupa wal ituamakkenaeye.
pupa wala sermesena, pupa kinnenaeye.
kirpar onoet iwalapaliye.   140
kirpala nikka ilekuet iwalapaliye.
nele ukkupana yapi sailakan attikwichi.
yapi sailakanti pioklekwichiye.
nele ukkupana yapi sailakanakwa iipyekwakwichiye.
pel olo iispele.   145
olo yapi sailakan iipyamakkekwakwichiye.
yapi sailakan aitakkarmakkekwakwichiye.
nele ukkupana yapi sailakantinaye.
imakkekwakwichi unni tule pal ittoelesuliye.
pela kalili kwaleye.   150
yapi sailakan imakkekwakwichiye.
pela tunu pilu kwaleye yapi sailakan imakkekwakwichiye.
pela tar tar kwenaleye, tar tar kwenaleye.
yapi sailakan imakkekwakwichiye.
pela olo wachi kwaleye.   155
olo wachi nupurwi kwaleye.
nele ukkupana yapi sailakan imakkekwakwichiye.
unni tar pal ittoelesuliye.
yapi sailakan aitattamakkekwakwichiye.
pela kappana kwaleye, kappana kia kwaleye.   160
yapi sailakan imakkekwichi pela tarkwenale tarkwenaleye.
nele ukkunpana yapi sailakan imakkekwakwichiye.
pelaye wachi kwale olo wachi nupurwi kwaleye.

If I disappear myself from you for four days you see.   120
If I myself suffer you see say.
In the other abodes of the owners of chicha.
If they compete with (doubt) (the power of) my knower.
Then I will attack back" is what I say.
Sacred Ukkupana is addressing (his spouse).   125
"There are owners of chicha who will compete with my knower.
If with the enemy people's ritual rifle.
They flame (shoot) at my body at mine, at my skin mine say.
If they transform my skin into a sieve (shoot me full of holes) say.
If they extinguish my vision (eyes) (= kill me) you see say.   130
I will disappear myself from you for four days."
He is standing calling out one more time to his spouse.
"If the owners of chicha cut my skin into pieces you see.
I will attack the owners of chicha right back" is what he says.
"To the sixth level (underground) tiny, vines (snakes = troops) for the
    owners.   135
I will go and command."
Sacred Ukkupana is standing calling one more time to his spouse.
Sacred Ukkupana Sure Shot Man goes and steps himself forward.
He goes and drifts himself away, he goes and speeds himself along
    quickly.
Along the path of obtaining aliment.   140
Along the path of animal aliment.
Sacred Ukkupana's principal portals are standing closed.
The principal portals are standing nailed.
Sacred Ukkupana's principal portals are standing reflecting.
Like a golden mirror.   145
The golden principal portals are standing reflecting like stars.
The principal portals are standing reflecting all over.
And Sacred Ukkupana's principal portals.
Are standing sounding the different tones cannot be distinguished.
All like *kalili* bugs.   150
The principal portals are standing sounding.
All like *pilu pilu* bugs the principal portals are standing sounding.
All in different ways, in different ways.
The principal portals are standing sounding.
All like golden clocks.   155
Like golden baby clocks (pocket watches).
Sacred Ukkupana's principal portals are standing sounding.
The different tones cannot be distinguished.
The principal portals are standing chiming.
All like bells, like tiny bells.   160
The principal portals are standing sounding all differently all differently.
Sacred Ukkunpana's principal entrances are standing sounding.
All like clocks like golden baby clocks.

pela kittali kwaleye yapi sailakan imakkekwakwichiye.
pela tar tar kwenale tar tar kwenaleye.   165
yapi sailakan imakkekwakwichiye.
pelaye nele takkwili kwaleye.
yapi sailakan uurmakkekwakwichi.
unni tule tar pali ittosatopisuliye.
nele ukkupana yapi tarpa noenae.   170
yapi tarpa noekwakwichi.
neka talepa nekasekaye.
nele ukkupana yapi tarpa noenae.
olo puti pali takka kwaleye.
olo siku tukku pali takka kwaleye.   175
nele ukkupana kinki tule tula nelekan nik kolekwakwichiye.
neka pilli nerkwa nerkwakine.
kalu tokia pilli akkarpiye.
tula nelekanse nappi kolekwichiye.
ina napkakkali kia tupakan ainakkwenanaiye.   180
topele topele pela kaipile kaipileye.
pela wiasali kwale kalu poomakkenai.
kalu etarpenanaiye.
tula nelekan ainakkwenanaiye.
pela pipinyale pipinyale tula nelekan ainakkwenanaiye.   185
neka kunasu pillisekaye.
tula nelekan ainakkwenanai.
tula nelekan nik kolekwichikusaye.
tula nele kia tupakan ainakkwenanai.
kalukwa saila akkarpiye.   190
eka tummatika kuemaitti posumpase.
na kolekwakwichikusa nekati kunasu pillikineye.
ina tula nele sampulakkwa na kia tupaye.
sunna kolekwanaikusaye.
pela kaipile kaipile, pela wiasalikwaleye.   195
kalu sattatiena, kalu poomakkenanaiye.
tula nelekan ainakkwenanai.
neka kunasu pillise.
tula nelekan ainakkwenanaiye.
"kirpalapa penekuali" sokele.   200
"kirpalati tule kinkin tule" tar sokemoiniye.

All like accordions the principal entrances are standing sounding.
All differently all differently. 165
The principal entrances are standing sounding.
All like sacred thunder.
The principal portals are standing roaring.
The different tones could not be distinguished.
Sacred Ukkupana goes and leaves through the portal. 170
He is standing leaving through the portal.
Outside of the house beside the house.
Sacred Ukkupana goes and leaves through the portal.
He prepares his golden blowgun.
He prepares the point of his golden arrow. 175
Sacred Ukkupana Sure Shot Man is standing calling directly to the live
    sacred medicines.
At the sixth level the sixth one.
Up to the very Tokia (name) stronghold level.
He is standing calling one more time to the sacred medicines.
The tiny *napkiar* (medicinal plant) vines are going along climbing up. 180
Frightened frightened (by the taste) all bitter bitter.
All like dripping rain the stronghold is misty.
Going along watching taking care of the stronghold.
The sacred medicines are going along climbing up.
All changing form changing form (appearing and disappearing) the
    sacred medicines are going along climbing up. 185
On top of the house on top of the place.
The sacred medicines are going along climbing up.
He (Sacred Ukkupana) was standing calling directly to the sacred
    medicines.
The sacred medicine vines are going along climbing up.
To the very foundation of their stronghold. 190
To the abode of their leader.
He (Sacred Ukkupana) was standing calling above the house the place.
The sacred *sampulakkwa* vine medicine.
He was truly calling (to it).
All bitter bitter, all like dripping rain. 195
The stronghold is covered with clouds, the stronghold is all misty.
The sacred medicines are going along climbing up.
Above the house the place.
The sacred medicines are going along climbing up.
 "When we begin to compete with the aliment" he says. 200
"The aliment man (other snakes) is a sure shot man" he says.

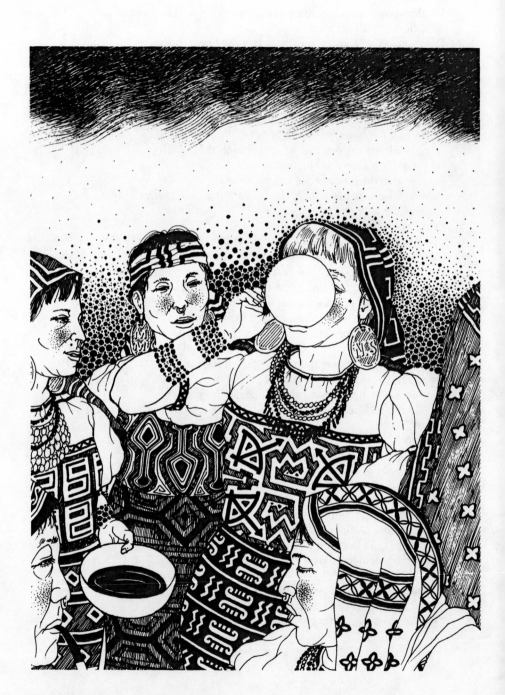

Figure 16. Women drinking chicha during puberty festivities

Chapter 9

The Way of Making Chicha

Performed by Mastaletat

Inna sopet ikar /The Way of Making Chicha was performed by Chief Mastaletat of Mulatuppu on April 27, 1970. At the time, Mastaletat was one of the primary chiefs of the village of Mulatuppu. Intelligent and friendly, Chief Mastaletat was very knowledgeable of Kuna tradition. In addition to myths and history, he was a great storyteller, appreciated by audiences not only in his own village, but throughout Kuna Yala. I often traveled with him to other villages where people loved to hear him talk and chant.

Mastaletat was also a specialist in the preparation of *inna* "chicha," the fermented drink consumed in large quantities at girls' puberty rites. In addition to knowing how to prepare chicha physically, he knew and it was his duty to perform the chants associated with and necessary to successful preparation, such as *The Way of Making Chicha*. Chief Mastaletat was a Kuna bon vivant. He was always lively and full of good spirits. While he never drank otherwise, he drank a lot during the puberty rites in which he was involved.

Like other magical chants, *The Way of Making Chicha* is addressed to representatives of the spirit world, in this case those of the fermenting fruits, plants, and other ingredients that are used in the making of chicha. It is performed while the chicha is in the process of fermenting. This long chant, the longest in this book, is a beautiful narrative description of not only the making of the chicha, but also related events, such as the participation of the entire Kuna village in the rites and festivities. It is by means of the performance of *The Way of Making Chicha* that Mastaletat assures that the chicha will be made properly and that associated ritual activities will occur as they are supposed to.

The Way of Making Chicha describes in remarkable detail and with incredible precision the events associated with Kuna puberty rites, and

for this reason alone is an extremely valuable ethnographic and histori-
cal document. When Kuna parents (called here the "owners of chicha")
decide to sponsor an *inna* "chicha" for their daughter, they go to the
specialist and ask him to prepare chicha. The specialist, the *inna sopet*
"chicha maker," called the *tuu sopa yai* "libation maker" in the text,
agrees and prepares to carry out his task. He and his wife bathe and get
dressed in their finest attire for the events to follow. He confers with his
assistants and goes to the chicha house, where the beverage is made and
consumed.

In the chicha house the chicha specialist directs all activities. Special
pots are lined up for making the chicha. Sugarcane, bananas, and other
plants are ground and boiled. The chicha specialist chants to the spirits
of these plants so that they ferment properly. His chanting is described
metaphorically as "gathering heart." This chant is actually *The Way of
Making Chicha*, the very chant represented here.

During the preparation of the chicha, the chicha specialist converses
with the sponsors of the event and tastes the chicha to decide when it will
be ready. The tasting is an elaborate ritual, the Kuna equivalent of French
wine tasting. Little by little inhabitants of other villages (called uncles)
arrive in order to participate in the ritual and festivities. The sponsors of
the ritual get ready for it and converse with the chicha specialist. There
is more and more activity as the festivities get going. The chant describes
the various participants, their clothing (ties, hats, molas), jewelry (gold
and silver necklaces, native beads), makeup (red dye from a jungle plant),
and movements, and the ritual objects, such as hammocks, drinking cups,
and musical instruments, they put in place and use; the increasing inter-
play of talk, laughter, and noise; and the actual drinking and inebriation.
The different moments and aspects of the narrative do not follow the kind
of linear logic to which most readers of this book are probably accustomed. Rather they intersect, intermingle, and overlap in a very Kuna
expression of the symbolic and magical nature of their puberty ritual.

GRAMMAR, PARALLELISM, VOCABULARY

As all Kuna magical chants, *The Way of Making Chicha* has grammatical features that distinguish it from everyday speech as well as from other
Kuna verbal and literary genres. In particular this chant employs a large
set of verbal suffixes that indicate in intricate detail the position, motion,
movement, direction, and timing of activities. Again as in other magical
chants, the optative final suffix *-ye* is omnipresent, marking line endings

and providing a mystical, optative tone to the chant. Morphemes typically occur in their long form, containing a final vowel that is usually deleted in everyday speech.

Descriptive detail as well as overall length is also achieved through extensive parallelism. Parallel lines describe people getting dressed, moving, bathing, and conversing; various activities; and sounds and noises.

Their sacred clothing.
Their work clothing.
Their head kerchief clothing.
They are standing changing them.

And the owners of chicha.
They are standing putting on their golden neckties.
They are standing changing their golden hats.
Before going to see the abode of the libation maker.

They went to stand themselves there in the lap of the river.
They were making waves in the lap of the river.
In the very lap of the river they are making waves.
In the very lap of the river they were moving about.
In the very lap of the river they were splashing.

The libation maker is now announcing.
"Did you gather enough Sister Golden Osilisopteye (spirit name
    of sweet juice made from banana) for me?" he says.
"Yes we gathered enough Sister Golden Osilisopteye for you, for
    this reason we have come."
The owners of chicha announce to the libation maker they do.

Under the enemy's pots.
The sacred fire is flaming.
The sacred fire is flaming out.
The sacred fire is sparkling.
Beneath the enemy's pots.

He lay strengthening the very libation vessels (the liquid in
    them).
He is fortifying the very libation vessels.
He is making sour (ferment) the very libation vessels.

The owners of chicha are filling the place with sound.
They are filling the place with noise.

Pairs of lines and stanzalike groups of lines are repeated frequently.

She sways herself along.
She steps herself along.
She moves herself back and forth.
Toward the abode the house.

They are getting valiant for the libation.
They are getting fortified for the libation.

The libation maker was sitting watching over this.
Within the libation place the house.

The Way of Making Chicha is a reflection and expression of the rich and complex vocabulary of the Kuna language. Many words in this chant are esoteric in that they are quite different from the everyday Kuna words for the object, activity, plant, or individual they describe. They are clearly a central aspect of the poetry of this text. In order to convey a sense of the Kuna performance, I have translated these words into an esoteric and poetic English, remaining as close to the original Kuna as possible. Thus I use "owners of chicha" for "Kuna people"; "spouse" for "wife"; "sound out" and "announce" for "speak"; "abode" for "house"; "sway along," "step along," and "move back and forth" for various Kuna movements; and "libation" for "chicha." Sometimes everyday and esoteric words are used side by side, as in *e posumpa nekaki* "in his abode his house" or *tuu inna ipekana imayteye* "the owners of the libation the chicha sound out."

Some of the words in the text can be understood only in terms of Kuna social and cultural practice and beliefs, as well as history. Kuna people are metaphorically called "owners of chicha" because they are, especially with regard to the event described in *The Way of Making Chicha*, literally the owners of this beverage. Spirits of the fermenting plants and fruits, as well as other sacred objects used in the puberty ritual, are considered by the Kuna to be humanlike—they have names, wear clothes, talk, and have chiefs, who lead them in their various tasks. The pots used to make the chicha are called "enemy pots." This means that they are not native to or made by the Kuna themselves, but are purchased from the outside, from Colombians or Panamanians, former enemies of the Kuna. Drinking chicha, in this and other texts in this book, is called "competing" with chicha. Drinkers compete with the chicha itself, to see if they can finish a full cup, as well as with others, to see if they can outlast them.

Olokwagdi de Akwanusadup's first illustration for *The Way of Making Chicha* "Chanting to the chicha" (fig. 13, p. 95), shows a specialist in the making of chicha, like Mastaletat, sitting in front of a pot of fermenting chicha, chanting to the spirits of the plants used in the fermentation process. Beside him he (and we) imagine the *kantules* (masters of ceremonies of the puberty rites) performing their ritual chant. They wear their special feathered hats, play sacred flutes, and shake sacred rattles. One of my photographs (photo 15) also shows this event. Olokwagdi's other illustration for this chant, "Women drinking chicha during puberty festivities" (fig. 16, p. 146) shows Kuna women, in their finest attire, headkerchiefs, molas, skirts, beads, noserings and earrings, and native dye makeup on their cheeks, happily drinking large quantities of chicha. The woman in the bottom left can be seen smoking a pipe.

My photographs show some of the many activities that occur during puberty rites (photos 10–21). These include a women and men grinding sugarcane in order to make chicha, the preparation of chicha, chicha fermenting in pots, *kantules* performing, the playing of long flutes, women preparing and men and women eating ritual meals, and the preparation of a special hammock for the ritual.

Here is *The Way of Making Chicha*, as performed by Mastaletat.

Kuna

inna ipekana imayteye.
tuu inna ipekana imayteye.
"tuu sopa yaiti takkenaele kepe suliwaye."

uu molaye.
uukana molaye.   5
nailaki molaye.
ulukwakekwichiye.

uu molaye.
uukana molaye.
narpisu molaye.   10
ulukwakekwichiye.

uu molaye.
uukanna molaye.
muswena molaye.
ulukwakekwichiye.   15
kana apisua posumpa takket ituaye.

inna ipekantinaye.
olo korpattanakampi naisikkekwichiye.
olo kurkinapi kwakekwichiye.
tuu sopa yai posumpa takket ituaye.   20

pupa wala na aipatteye.
pupa wala na ituamayteye.
pupa wala na kaswamayteye.
tuu sopa yai posumpa iwala paliye.

inna ipe alulu saila naka paliye.   25
tuu sopa yai walepunkwaye pupa na aitikesiiye.
"pe tuu sopa yaite, pia kuekwichiye pete takketeye?"

"ani tuu sopa yaiteye.
e posumpa nekakiye, pupa na aitikemaiye.
tala pinyemaiye tala ikaemaiye."   30

tuu sopa yaiye walepunkwaye pupa wala ituamayteye.
pupa wala muchuppimayteye.
pupa wala na kaswamayteye.

tuu sopa yaiye posumpaye.

English

The owners of chicha (Kuna persons) sound out.
The owners of the libation the chicha sound out.
"Let us go and see the libation maker."

Their sacred clothing.
Their sacred work clothing.   5
Their striped clothing.
They are standing changing them.

Their sacred clothing.
Their sacred work clothing.
Their curvy figured clothing.   10
They are standing changing them.

Their sacred clothing.
Their work clothing.
Their head kerchief clothing.
They are standing changing them.   15
Before going to see the abode of the knower the specialist.

And the owners of chicha.
They are standing putting on their golden neckties.
They are standing changing their golden hats.
Before going to see the abode of the libation maker.   20

They sway themselves along.
They step themselves now along.
They move themselves along.
Toward the path of the abode of the libation maker.

Beside the owner of chicha's sacred fireplace.   25
The spouse of the libation maker is now sitting.
(The owner of chicha asks) "Your libation maker, where is he standing
    do you think?"

"My libation maker.
Is now himself lying, in his abode his house.
His vision is lying turning around his vision is lying illuminating."   30

The spouse of the libation maker steps herself along.
She moves herself back and forth.
She now moves herself along.

The abode of the libation maker.

yapi palimesekwichiye.   35
e posumpa yapi sailakanti uurmayteye.
kulile kulile.
e posumpa yapi sailakanti, imayteye.

tuu sopa yai posumpa yapi saila opiekwichiye.
tuu sopa yai posumpa yapi saila, pal opiamakkekwichiye.   40
tuu sopa yai, e posumpa yapi saila pal attikwichiye.

pupa wala na aipatteye.
pupa wala ituamayteye.
pupa wala na muchuppimayteye.
e posumpa nekasekaye.   45

tuu sopa yaiti, uu kachiki aitikemaiye.
inna ipekantiye.
se wakkila kunikkiye.

"ipi sunna waye panse wakkila kunnikki teeye?"
tuu sopa yai na palimaiye maiye.   50
inna ipekansekaye.

"panka tuuti wimakke pierpaye naka pe takkeye."
inna ipekante tuu sopa yaika palimaye kwichiye.

tuu sopa yai na palimakkialiye.
"puna olo osilisopteye panka unnimaysa?" sokewa.   55
"puna olo osilisopte peka unnimaysawa, an soke tanikkiye."
inna ipekante tuu sopa yaika palimaye kuaye.

tuu sopa yai na palimaye "napi" soke iniye.
"peka aku takkele kepe suliwa."
inna ipekanka na palimaye kuaye.   60

tuu sopa yai na palimakkialiye.
"kepe ilakwen takkeye kep an ipi sokewa.
ante kusaku saetti inna ipekankala."
tuu sopa yaiti na palimakkialiye.

She is standing pushing the portal. 35
The principal portal of the abode makes noise.
Like the *kuli* flute the *kuli* flute.
The principal portal of the abode, sounds out.

She is standing crossing the principal portal of the abode of the libation
  maker.
She is standing crossing again, the principal portal of the abode of the
  libation maker. 40
She is standing, closing again the principal portal of the abode of the
  libation maker.

She sways herself along.
She steps herself along.
She moves herself back and forth.
Toward the abode the house. 45

The libation maker, is lying in his sacred hammock.
The owners of chicha.
Present themselves to him.

"For what reason do you present yourselves to me?"
The libation maker is lying announcing he is. 50
To the owners of chicha.

"We come to ask you to sweat out (make) the libation for this reason
  you see."
The owners of chicha are standing announcing to the libation maker.

The libation maker is now announcing.
"Did you gather enough Sister Golden Osilisopteye (spirit name of
  sweet juice made from banana) for me?" he says. 55
"Yes we gathered enough Sister Golden Osilisopteye for you, for this
  reason we have come."
The owners of chicha announce to the libation maker they do.

The libation maker now announces "It is good" he says he does.
"I have to see for you now."
He announces now to the owners of chicha he does. 60

The libation maker now is announcing.
"This is not the first time I do this say.
I have always done this for the owners of chicha."
The libation maker now is announcing.

machi inna ittoappilelese itakkemekwisaye.   65
yala yala palimalattise itakkemekwisa.
nase itakkemalattiseye.

inna ipekantiye.
"napi" sokeiniye.
inna ipekanti tuu sopa yai posumpa nekaki pup aipilialiye.   70
pup na aipiryekwichi.
tuu sopa yai posumpa yapi saila palimesekwichi.
tuu sopa yai posumpa yapi sailakan imayteye.
tuu sopa yai posumpa yapi sailakan aitattamayteye.
unni ukakka pal ittokelesuliye.   75

inna ipekan tuu sopa yaiye.
inna ipekanteye.
e walepunkwa na palimayeye.
"iki peka soke?" "ini 'napi' sokeini.
'aku takkele kepe suliwaliye.'   80
tuu sopa yai na palimaye kuanaye."

tuu sopa yaitiye, neka ulu akku maitetipaliye.
neka kupyaleketipaliye.
tuu sopa yaiti kapi kiali saemekwisaye.
pupa pali wisikusapiesuliye.   85

tuu sopa yaitinaye.
"ulukkana pok tuleye panki waka piokkaliye."
pupa walaye ko pupa wala.
pali wisikusapie.
e walepunkwa pupa pali wisikusapiesuliye.   90

tuu sopa yaiti.
pupa na attaaliye.
pule kokoli pap walakanti, ulukkana palimakkialiye.
inna ipekanti neka pillipi tuloaliye.
neka pilliti waitikkoaliye.   95
puna olo osilisopte ulekwirmakkenanai, inna ipekantinaye.

tuu sopa yaitiye nase itakkemalattiseye.
nase itakkemai yala yalapalimalatti.
machi inna ittoappilelese nase itakkemaiye.

He conferred with the chicha tasting boys (assistants of the libation
    maker).   65
He conferred with his followers.
With his conferees.

The owners of chicha.
"It is good" they say.
The owners of chicha are twirling themselves away from the abode the
    house of the libation maker.   70
They are now standing twirling themselves around.
They are standing pushing the principal portal of the abode of the
    libation maker.
The principal portal of the abode of the libation maker sounds out.
The principal portal of the abode of the libation maker makes sounds.
Its different tones cannot be distinguished.   75

The owners of chicha (leave the house) of the libation maker.
The owners of chicha.
Their spouses now announce.
"What does he (the libation maker) say to you?" "'It is good' he says.
'I have to see first for you.'   80
The libation maker now announces he does."

And the libation maker, since the day (sun) has faded again.
The day has become dark again.
The libation maker is sleeping he lay down he did.
His body no longer felt anything.   85

And the libation maker (he says).
"The crowing winged person (cock) is pecking (crowing) for me."
His body his body.
No longer felt anything.
His spouse's body did not feel anything either.   90

The libation maker.
Now is waking himself up.
The crowing winged ones (cocks), are announcing.
The owners of chicha are filling the place with sound.
They are filling the place with noise.   95
The owners of chicha are going about grinding, Sister Golden
    Osilisopteye.

The libation maker is with his conferees.
He is conferring with his followers.
He is lying conferring with the chicha tasting boys.

e walepunkwakana palimayeye.   100
"uu molaye, uukkana mola nailaki mola, ulukwakekwichiye.
ia wala nukkuse apalukkenaemala."
ia wala nukkuseye pupa wala kwichikutappiye.
ia wala nukku omuryenaikusaye.
ia wala nukkupi omuryena.   105
ia wala nukkupi sukkamakkenaikusaye.
ia wala nukkupi epikenaikusaye.
ia wala tulaki tolakampi.
saylikiapi maymakkoe take.
saylikiapi okaryenaikusaye.   110

ipe itukka pilli nukkuse pupa kwichikunikki.
tuu sopa yai e walepunkwaye.
ia wala nukkuki apalukkenaikusamokainiye.
ia wala omuryenaikusamoiniye.
ia walapi osukkamakkenaikusamoiniye.   115
ia wala nukkuki, ia wala tulaki tolakampi saylikiapi
    maymakkoenaikusamoiniye.
tuu sopa yai e walepunkwa ia wala pillise pal ainakkwekwichimoiniye.

tuu sopa yaiti pupa wala ituamayteye.
pupa wala muchuppimayteye.
pupa wala na kaswamayteye.   120
tuu sopa yai e posumpa yapi saila palimesekwichiye.
tuu sopa yai posumpa yapi tarpa tokekwichiye.
inna ipekan imayteye.
"olo kana we yapa kanakante oilimakkomalarkeye.
mani kana we yapa kanakanteye.   125
oilimakkomalarkeye."
tuu sopa yaite olo kana we yapa kanakanki, pupa na marwetappiye.
mani kana we yapa kanakanki.
pupa marwetappiye.
olo kana maisu ina pillikanki.   130
pupa wala marwitappiye.

tuu sopa yai neka palitakkesikwisaye.
tuu kunaye posumpa nekakineye.

inna ipekantinaye.
pila tolaye esmette poakikampi, ilemayteye.   135
ile ilepo naaleye.
pila tol esmette poakikampi, ilemakkenasaye.

Their spouses announce.   100
"Stand changing, your sacred clothing your sacred work clothing,
    your striped clothing.
Let's go and bathe in the lap of the river."
They went to stand themselves there in the lap of the river.
They were making waves in the lap of the river.
In the very lap of the river they are making waves.   105
In the very lap of the river they were moving about.
In the very lap of the river they were splashing.
The river sardines.
Come to leave their smell in their very hair.
Their very hair was floating.   110

She is standing herself at the lap of the mouth of the river.
The spouse of the libation maker.
She was also bathing in the lap of the river.
She was also making waves in the river.
She was also moving about in the very river.   115
In the lap of the river, the river sardines were leaving their smell in her
    very hair.
The spouse of the libation maker is also standing climbing up the bank
    of the river again.

The libation maker steps himself along.
He moves himself back and forth.
He now moves himself along.   120
The libation maker is standing pushing the principal portal of his abode.
The libation maker is standing entering the principal portal of his abode.
The owners of chicha sound out.
"The golden benches let us order the benches there in line.
The silver benches there the benches.   125
Let us order them in line."
The libation maker sat himself down, on the golden benches there the
    benches.
On the silver benches there the benches.
He sat himself down there.
(The assistants) on the golden benches the sacred side ones.   130
Sat themselves down there.

The libation maker was sitting watching over this.
Within the libation place the abode the house.

The owners of chicha.
Line up the enemy's (foreigner's), very pots.   135
In two lines they do.
They were lining up, the enemy's pots.

puna olo kaypikintilikampa aisurmakkemaiye.
pila tol esmette poakikankineye.

pila tola esmette poakikankineye.   140
puna olo kaypikintili.
enosattikineye.
alimaisattikineye.

inna ipekan walepunkanaye.
inna ipekan walepunkanaye.   145
ipe alu sailakampi uurpialiye.
pila tol esmette poakikankineye.

pila tol esmette poakikannaka pali.
ipe alulu sailakanti kwapunnualiye.
ipe alulu sailakanti takkarmakkaliiye.   150
ipe alulu sailakanti tittismakkaliye.
pila tol esmette poakikankineye.

pila tol esmette poakikankineye.
puna olo kaypikintilikan ainakkwialiye.
e makkulakan ainakkwenanaiye.   155
esmette pila tol esmetteye pillipillikineye.

inna ipekan walepunkanaye.
oukarpa totokkwakampi, onakkwialiye.
inna pila tolaye, walepunkanaye.

inna ipekan walepunkanaye.   160
pila tola esmette poakikampi tittilamakkaliye.
pila tol esmette poakikampi tittilamakkenasa.
pila tola olo puna olo kaypikintilikantinaye.

pila tol inna ipekan walepunkan imayteye.
ukakka pal ittokelesuliye.   165
inna ipekan walepunkan imayteye.

tuu sopa yaitina palimakkialiye.
"pun olo kaypikintili e apalisakante panki sayetakemala."
puna olo kaypikintili e apalisakante, pal ittotoaliye.
tuu sopa yaitinaye.   170

puna olo kaypikintili, e apalisakante pal ittotosattikineye.
inna ipekanse na palimakkialiye.

They are emptying Sister Golden Kaypikintili (spirit of sweet juice made
    from sugarcane).
Into the enemy's pots.

The enemy's pots.   140
With Sister Golden Kaypikintili.
Are filled.
Are full.

The spouses of the owners of chicha.
The spouses of the owners of chicha.   145
Are placing sacred fire.
Beneath the enemy's pots.

Under the enemy's pots.
The sacred fire is flaming.
The sacred fire is flaming out.   150
The sacred fire is sparkling.
Beneath the enemy's pots.

Within the enemy's pots.
Sister Golden Kaypikintili is rising (boiling).
Her foam is going along rising up.   155
Toward the very edge of the enemy's pots the pots.

The spouses of the owners of chicha.
Are raising up, the tiny sacred baskets (attached to a long pole and used
    to skim off foam).
The spouses, the enemy's chicha (pots).

The spouses of the owners of chicha.   160
Are straining the enemy's pots.
They are in the process of straining the enemy's pots.
The enemy's (pots of) Sister Golden Kaypikintili.

The spouses of the owners of the enemy's chicha sound out.
Their different voices cannot be distinguished.   165
The spouses of the owners of chicha sound out.

And the libation maker is announcing.
"Bring to me the juices of Sister Golden Kaypikintili."
He is tasting once more, the juices of Sister Golden Kaypikintili.
The libation maker.   170

Having tasted once more the juices, of Sister Golden Kaypikintili.
He is announcing to the owners of chicha.

"puna olo kaypikintili e apalisakanaye.
pal ittotosattikineye."

inna ipekan imayteye.   175
"ipe na pormokkinakampi panki sayetakemala.
puna olo kaypikintili, e apalisakampi weyenanai," inna ipekantinaye.

ikwa ulu suise pal aisurmakkemaiye.
pila tol esmette poakikanti pal aiteyemaiye.
pila tola esmette poakikampi, pal ainakkwemaiye.   180

inna ipekantinaye.
pila tol esmette poakikanki, pal aitesattikineye.
inna ipekantina.
inna ipekante pal osukkuamakkenanaiye.
pali otiop saenanaiye, inna ipekantinaye.   185

inna ipekantinaye.
"kulili poomettekanteye.
panki oteetakemala.
inna pomettekanaye, nukakwal aiteketakeye."
tuu sopa yaiti palimakkialiye.   190

tuu sopa yai na palimakkialiye.
"aitaryana pomettenakampi otekenanaiye.
aitaryana pomettekampi ulukkenanai.
inna pomettekampi, ewaryenanaiye," inna ipekantinaye.

"orokkwana pomettenakampi otekenanaiye."   195

orokkwana pomettenakampi otetemalattikine.
api ururukkenanai, inna ipekanti naye.

tirpikkwana pomettenakampi otekenanaiye.
tirpikkwana pomettenakampi ewaryenana, inna ipekantinaye.

inna pomettenakampi mu tikenanaiye.   200
mu olo tar kaluye mu napaliye.

inna pomettenakanti ilemakkenasaye.
mu olo tar kalu mu napali.
ile ilepo naale.
tuu pomettenakanti ilemakkenasaye.   205

"The juices of Sister Golden Kaypikintili.
I have tasted them all once more."

The owners of chicha sound out.   175
"Bring us here now the sacred buckets.
To be going along dipping up the very juices of, Sister Golden
    Kaypikintili," the owners of chicha (say).

They are emptying it into the pirogue of *ikwa* wood.
They are lowering again the enemy's pots.
They are raising again, the enemy's pots.   180

And the owners of chicha.
Having lowered again, the enemy's very pots.
The owners of chicha.
The owners of chicha are again going along stirring it (to make it cool).
They are again going along making it cool, the owners of chicha.   185

And the owners of chicha.
"The *kulili* (angular in form) vessel.
Lower it for me.
Lower all, the chicha vessels by name."
The libation maker is announcing.   190

The libation maker is now announcing.
"Be going about lowering the *aitaryana* (flat, falling in form) vessels.
Be going about rinsing the *aitaryana* vessels.
Be going about cleansing, the chicha vessels," (he says to) the owners of
    chicha.

"Be going about lowering the *orokkwana* (round in form) vessels."   195

Having lowered the *orokkwana* vessels.
Having been going about rinsing the very ones, the owners of chicha
    leave.

They go about lowering the *tirpikkwana* (circular in form) vessels.
They go about cleansing the *tirpikkwana* vessels, the owners of chicha.

They go about digging a hole (in the ground) for the chicha vessels.   200
Along the golden wall.

They went about lining up the chicha vessels.
Along the golden wall.
They made two lines.
They went about lining up the chicha vessels.   205

inna pomettekankineye, puna olo kaypikintilikanti, aisuurmakkaliye.
inna ipekante puna olo kaypikintilikampi pali sayenanaiye.

inna pomettenakanti enamaysattikineye, inna pomettekan
   alimaysattikineye.
esaliki urwanaki saktileali.
esaliki urwanaki saktilekesikwisa.   210
witillete naye mu olo tar kaluye mu napali kuaye.

pela saktilesattikine inna ipekana, tuu sopa yaikana, palimakkialiye.
"ipekala kunpikwaye panka wiluppukana naisikkeye?"
"ipekala kunnerkwaye wiluppukana peka naisikke an sokeye."
tuu sopa yai na palimakkialiye.   215

inna tuu inna ipekantina palimakkiali, "napi" sokeiniye.
"ipe matturu walakanteye.
ipekala kunpikwa naale.
ante wiluppukana naisikke?" soke kuaye.

tuu sopa yaina, palimakkiali "ipekala kunpakke naale.   220
ipe matturu, walakanteye, pali wis siyto kuaye.
man ayla pillikante enamaytoe.
man ayla pillikante akkimaytoeye."
tuu sopa yaina palimakkialiye.

tuu sopa yaitina pupa na aipatteye.   225
pupa na seleteye.
pupa na ituamayteye.
e posumpa nekasekaye.

e posumpaseye na pupa naye kwichikutappiye.
tuu sopa yai e walepunkwa na palimakkialiye.   230
"inna ipekanka iki wiluppukana pe naisiysa?"
"ipekala kunnerkwa wiluppukana naisiysa."
e walepunkwa "napi" sokeiniye.
"ante tuu pakkana penekuemo" ipi sokewa.
tuu sopa yai, e walepunkwa na palimayeye.   235

tuu sopa yaiti neka ulu wakku maitetipaliye.
neka ulu kupyaletetipali.
tuu sopa yaitiye.
kweki tup otimakkemekwisa.
tuu sopa yaina palimakkialiye.   240

They are emptying, Sister Golden Kaypikintilikanti, into the chicha
vessels.
The owners of chicha go about carrying Sister Golden Kaypikintilikampi
once more.

Having filled the chicha vessels, the chicha vessels were full.
They are sealing them with *urwa* leaves.
They were sealed with *urwa* leaves.   210
Attached along the golden wall they were.

When all was sealed the owners of chicha, are announcing, to the
libation maker.
"For how many days time period will you wait?"
"For six days time period I will wait for you."
The libation maker is now announcing.   215

And the owners of chicha of the libation of chicha are announcing,
"It is good" they say.
"The sacred ripe ones (plantains).
In how many days.
Do we need to get them?" they say they do.

The libation maker, is announcing "In four days.   220
You must cut, the sacred ripe, ones.
You must fill up the silver shelves.
And then empty the silver shelves."
The libation maker is announcing.

The libation maker now sways himself along.   225
He now drifts himself away.
He now steps himself along.
Toward his abode his house.

Now he went to stand himself there at his abode.
The spouse of the libation maker is now announcing.   230
"How long a time period did you hang (give) for the owners of chicha?"
"I hung a six day time period."
His spouse says "It is good."
"I also will compete with (drink) the libation" is what she says.
The spouse, of the libation maker now announces.   235

The libation maker when the day has faded again.
When the day has become dark again.
The libation maker.
He lay down gathering his heart (thinking, chanting).
The libation maker is announcing (chanting).   240

naa tilikkwa sailakanse na kweki tup otimakkemekwisa.
naa tilikkwa sailakanaye.
na kweki tup otimakkemekwisaye.

inna pomettekampi kannoemekwisaye.
inna pomettekampi seloaliye.   245
inna pomettekampi kaypimakkaliye.
tuu sopa yai na kweki tup otimakkemekwisaye.

tuu sopa yai na palimayemaiye.
kanna tilikkwa sailakanse kweki tup otimakkemekwisa.
kanna tilikkwa sailakanseye.   250
mola muryakwal ainakkwiali inna pomette solulupali.
e kanaye kweki tup otimakkemekwisaye.

tuu sopa yai na palimayemekwisaye.
wawarkwalikwa sailakanse na kweki tup otimakkemekwisaye.
inna sailakampi kannoemekwisa.   255
kilu panna tolakan itu.
inna sailakampi kannoemekwisa.
kilu panna tolakan tuki.
olo kastipir tolakan upoali.
mani sakkilakwal upoaliye.   260
olo kana maisu ina pillikampi, enamakkali.
tuu sopa yai na kweki tup otimakkemekwisaye.

mani kastipir tolakan upoaliye.
mani sakkilakwal upoali.
mani sakkilaturpakwar imakkaliye.   265
tuu kuna nekasekaye.
tuu pina machoali.
tuu pina kannoaliye.
olo kana maisu ina pillikan alimakkaliye.

tuu sopa yai na kweki tup otimakkemekwisa.   270
inna sailakampi kannoemekwisa.
kepe ilakwen takke kep ipi sokekwa.
kusaku na sae tina iniye kana kweki tup otimakkemekwisaye.

inna ipekan imayteye.
"wiluppukana wisi kuele kepe suliwaye."   275
inna ipekan imayteye.
inna ipekan uu mola, uukkana mola.

He lay gathering heart to the *naa* plant chiefs (spirit leaders, to make
   chicha stronger).
The *naa* plant chiefs.
He lay gathering heart.

He lay strengthening the very libation vessels (the liquid in them).
He is fortifying the very libation vessels.   245
He is making sour (ferment) the very libation vessels.
The libation maker now lay gathering his heart.

The libation maker is now lying announcing.
He lay gathering heart to the *kanna* plant chiefs.
To the *kanna* plant chiefs.   250
All clothed they are rising up from the bottom of the chicha vessels.
Their specialist lay gathering heart.

The libation maker now lay announcing.
He lay gathering heart to the *wawarkwa* plant chiefs.
He lay strengthening the very chiefs of chicha.   255
Before (the arrival) of uncles inhabitants of faraway towns.
He lay strengthening the very chiefs of the chicha.
For the uncles inhabitants of faraway towns.
The golden castle inhabitants are entering.
Wearing silver jewelry they are entering.   260
They are filling, the long golden benches the sacred side ones.
The libation maker now lay gathering heart.

The silver castle inhabitants are entering.
Wearing silver jewelry they are entering.
Wearing silver seeded jewelry they are doing it (entering).   265
To the libation place the house.
They are getting valiant for the libation (ready to drink chicha).
They are getting fortified for the libation.
They are filling up the long golden benches the sacred side ones.

The libation maker now lay gathering heart.   270
He lay strengthening the chiefs of the libation.
As he had done many times.
He had always now done thus the specialist lay gathering heart.

The owners of chicha sound out.
"We want to know after what time period we begin (the celebra-
   tion)."   275
The owners of chicha sound out.
The owners of chicha their sacred clothing, their sacred work clothing.

nailaki mola, ulukwakekwichiye.
tuu sopa yai, posumpa takketi ituaye.

inna ipekanaye, uu molaye.   280
narpisu molaye, ulukwakekwichiye.
ulu kurkinapi, kwakekwichiye.
tuu sopa yai, posumpa takket ituaye.

pupa wala na ituamayteye.
pupa wala muchuppimayteye.   285
pupa wala na kaswamayteye.
tuu sopa yai posumpaye nekasekaye.

tuu sopa yai posumpa yapi sailakana palimesekwichiye.
unni ukakka pal ittokele sunniye.

tuu sopa yai na pupa na aitikesiiye.   290
olo kana we yapa kana kanki pupa na aitikesiye.

tuu sopa yai na palimaye kuaye.
"ipi sunnaye, panse wakkila kunikkiye?"

tuu sopa yai, inna ipekan imayteye.
"ante ati inna ipekanteye.   295
tuu tiye ipekala kunnerkwa kusanainiye.
wiluppukana wisi kuele kepe suliwaye."

tuu sopa yai "napi" sokeiniye.
tuu sopa yai na palimakkialiye.
na yala yala palimalattiseye.   300
na inna ittoappileleseye, nase itakkemalattiseye.

pupa wala ituamayteye.
pupa wala muchuppimayteye.
pupa wala kaswamayteye.

tuu sopa tuu kuna posumpa yapi sailakanti palimesekwichiye.   305
tuu kuna posumpa yapi sailakanti, uurmayteye.
unni ukakka pal ittokelesuliye.

tuu kuna posumpa yapi tarpa tokekwichiye.
olo kana we yapa kanakampi ilimayteye.
mani kana we yapa kanakampi ilimayteye.   310

Their striped clothing, they are standing changing them.
Before going to see the abode, of the libation maker.

The owners of chicha, their sacred clothing.   280
Their curvy figured clothing, they are standing changing.
Their sacred hats, they are standing changing.
Before going to see the abode, of the libation maker.

They step themselves along.
They move themselves back and forth.   285
They move themselves along.
Toward the abode of the libation maker.

They are standing pushing the principal portal to the abode of the
    libation maker.
Its different tones cannot be distinguished.

The libation maker now is himself now sitting.   290
He is sitting on the golden bench there himself now on the bench.

The libation maker now announces he does.
"For what reason, do you present yourselves to me?"

The owners of chicha, sound out to the libation maker.
"It is we who are the owners of the chicha.   295
For the libation six days have passed.
We want to know after what time period we begin."

The libation maker says he does "It is true (time)."
The libation maker now is announcing.
Now to his followers.   300
Now to the chicha tasters, now to his conferees.

He steps himself along.
He moves himself back and forth.
He moves himself along.

The libation maker is standing pushing the principal portal of the
    libation place the abode.   305
The principal portal of the libation place the abode, makes noise.
Its different tones cannot be distinguished.

He is standing entering the principal portal of the libation place the
    abode.
The golden benches are lined up there.
The silver benches are lined up there.   310

olo kana we yapa kanakankiye.
tuu sopa yaiti, pupa marwitappiye.
mani kana we yapa kanakanki.
machi inna ittoappilele.
pupa marwitappiye.   315

nase itakkemalatti teeye.
olo kana maisu ina pillikankiye, pupa na marwitappiye.

tuu sopa yai inna ipekanseye, na palimakkialiye.
"ipe kakkururukkemalattiye, panki sayetakeye."
inna ipekanteye, ipe kakkururukkemalatti, api eyokekwichiye.   320

tuu sopa yaika ipe kakkururukkemalatti.
pali api ukkekwichiye.
tuu sopa yaitinaye, ipe kakkururukkemalatti, api ururukkesikwisaye.

tuu sopa yai na, palimakkiali.
inna ipekansekaye.   325
"puna olo kaypikintili, e apalisakante panki sayetakeye."

puna olo kaypinkintili, e apalisakante, pal ittotoaliye.
pal ittotoesikwisaye.

inna pomettekampi yallemakkaliye.
tuu sopa yaitinaye.   330
inna pomettekampi, yallemaysattikineye.
inna pomettenakanti, inikkimaysattikineye.

inna ipekanse na palimakkialiye.
"ipekala kunpaakwa, wiluppukana peka naisikkeye."
tuu sopa yai na palimakkialiye.   335

inna ipekan walepunkan imayteye, ukakka pal ittokelesuliye.
walepunkan allakwale, walepunkana piliteye.
unni ukakka pal ittokelesuliye.

"weki wiluppukana wisikuele kepe suliwaye."
walepunkan imayte kuaye.   340

The golden bench there on the golden bench.
The libation maker, went and sat himself down there.
The silver bench there on the silver bench.
The chicha tasting boys.
Went and sat themselves down there.   315

The conferees.
Went and sat themselves down there, on the long golden benches on the
    sacred side ones.

The libation maker now is announcing, to the owners of chicha.
"Bring me, the sacred mouth rinse."
The owners of chicha, are standing pouring, this very sacred mouth
    rinse for him.   320

For the libation maker the sacred mouth rinse.
They are standing giving it again to him.
And the libation maker, he was sitting rinsing his very mouth, with the
    sacred mouth rinse.

The libation maker now, is announcing.
To the owners of chicha.   325
"Bring me the juices, of Sister Golden Kaypikintili."

He is tasting again, the juices, of Sister Golden Kaypinkintili.
He was sitting tasting them again.

He is ordering (according to strength) the very chicha vessels.
And the libation maker.   330
Having ordered, the very chicha vessels.
Having lined up, the very chicha vessels.

He is now announcing to the owners of chicha.
"I hang for you (give you) three days, time period (before the
    celebration)."
The libation maker is now announcing.   335

The spouses of the owners of chicha sound out, their different tones
    cannot be distinguished.
The spouses all laugh, there are countless spouses.
Their different tones cannot be distinguished.

"We want to know for how long a time period (until we celebrate)."
The spouses sound out they do.   340

tuu sopa yaitiye.
pupa wala ituamayteye.
pupa wala muchuppimayteye.
pupa wala kaswamayteye.
e posumpa iwala paliye.   345

neka ulu akku maytetipaliye.
neka ulu kupyaletetipaliye.
neka uluye kupyaletetipaliye.
"ulukkana poy tuleye panki waka piokkaliye.
ulukka poy tuleye panki waka pioysattikineye."   350
inna sailakampi kannoemekwisaye.
inna sailakampi kaypimakkemekwisaye.
inna pomettekampi kaypimakkemekwisaye.
naa tilikkwa sailakan ainakkwialiye.
inna pomette pillisekaye.   355
e makkulakan ainakkwialiye.
e makkulakampiye, naikualiye.
inna pomette pillise pillise iniye.

kanna tilikkwa sailakan ainakkwialiye.
mola puryakwal ainakkwiali.   360
inna pomette pillipaliye.
mola kaypimakkakwal ainakkwiali.
mola tukku wala maisale.
kurkina wala maisale wala maisaleye.

naa tilikkwa sailakan ainakkwialiye.   365
mola puryakwal ainakkwiali.
inna pomette solulupa ainakkwialiye.
mola kaypimakkakwal ainakkwiali.
inna pomettekanti selekualiye.
inna pomettekanti kaypilealiye.   370
inna pomettekanti yopimakkaliye.

inna pomettenakantinaye.
tule kwau kwau ittoketi yopiye.
inna pomettekanti, kwaumakke pupukkwaye.
mu olo tar kaluye mu napaliye.   375

inna pomettenakantinaye.
inna pomette pillipaliye.
mola kaypimakkakwal, ainakkwialiye.

The libation maker.
He steps himself along.
He moves himself back and forth.
He moves himself along.
Toward his abode.   345

When the day has faded again.
When the day has become dark again.
When the day has indeed become dark again.
(The libation maker says) "The crowing winged person is pecking
    for me.
When the crowing winged person has finished pecking for me."   350
He lay strengthening the chiefs of the chicha.
He lay making sour the chiefs of the chicha.
He lay making sour the chicha vessels.
The *naa tilikkwa* plant chiefs are rising up.
On top of (at the mouth of) the chicha vessel.   355
Their foam is rising up.
Their very foam, is floating (on the liquid).
On top of on top of the chicha vessel.

The *kanna tilikkwa* plant chiefs are rising up.
All clothed they are rising up.   360
On top of the chicha vessel.
All clothed sour they are rising up.
Almost touching the point of their clothing (foam).
Almost touching the edges of their hats (points of foam).

The *naa tilikkwa* plant chiefs are rising up.   365
All clothed they are rising up.
They are rising up from the bottom of the chicha vessel.
All clothed sour they are rising up.
The chicha vessels (chicha) are getting fortified.
The chicha vessels are getting sour.   370
The chicha vessels are getting equal (same strength).

And the chicha vessels.
They sound the same as a newborn baby (crying).
The chicha vessels, all sound like newly borns.
Beside the sacred golden walls.   375

And the chicha vessels.
On top of the chicha vessels.
Clothed all sour, they are rising up.

inna pomettenakantinaye.
inna pomettekampi selekusattikineye.   380
inna pomettekampi, kaypilesattikineye.

tuu sopa yaiti, kapikiali saemekwisaye.
ulukka na pali wisikusapiesuliye.
e walepunkwa pali wisikusapiesuliye.

ipe ulukka kokopana saila ulukka na palimakkialiye.   385
tuu sopa yaitinaye.
pupa na attaali.
e walepunkwa na pupa attaali.
pupa war attakke mekwisaye.

tuu sopa yai na walepunkwase na palimakkialiye.   390
"uu molaye.
uu mola, uukkana mola, naila mola teye.
anka naisikke teye?"

inna ipekantinaye.
pila tola kupettu walapi, neka pilli tuloaliye.   395
ipe kupettu walapi.
neka pilli tuloemaiye.

tuu saila yaiti, uu mola uukkana mola.
narpisu mola, ulukwakekwichiye.
tuu pina kannoali.   400
tuu pina machoaliye.

tuu sopa yaitinaye.
olo kurkinapi kwakekwichiye.
olo korpattanakampi naisikkekwichiye.
tuu pina kannoali.   405
tuu pina machoaliye.

tuu sopa yai, e walepunkanaye.
tuu sopa yai walepunkanaye.
olo sakkilakwar naisikkaliye.
tuu pina kannoali.   410
tuu pina machoaliye.

tuu sopa yai walepunkanaye.
mani sakkilakwar, naisikkaliye.
inna ipekan, walepunkanaye.

As for the chicha vessels.
The chicha vessels are all fortified.   380
The chicha vessels, are all sour.

The libation maker, is falling asleep he did lie down.
His body did not feel anything.
His spouse did not feel anything either.

The sacred winged chief the winged one is now announcing.   385
And the libation maker.
He is now waking himself up.
His spouse is now waking herself up.
They lay waking themselves up.

The libation maker is now announcing now to his spouse.   390
"The sacred clothing.
The sacred clothing, the sacred work clothing, the striped clothing.
Where is it hanging for me?"

And the owners of chicha.
They are sounding out (shooting), the enemy's rifle (cannon).   395
The rifle.
Is sounding out.

The chiefs of the libation (people), their sacred clothing their sacred work
    clothing.
Their curvy figured clothing, they are standing changing.
They are getting fortified for the libation.   400
They are getting valiant for the libation.

And the libation maker.
He is standing changing his golden hat.
He is hanging (putting on) his golden tie.
He is getting fortified for the libation.   405
He is getting valiant for the libation.

And the spouses, of the libation maker (his and those of his assistants).
The spouses of the libation maker.
They are hanging on their golden necklaces.
They are getting fortified for the libation.   410
They are getting valiant for the libation.

The spouses of the libation maker.
They are hanging on, their silver necklaces.
The spouses, of the owners of chicha.

tuu pina kannoali.   415
tuu pina machoaliye.

inna ipekan walepunkanaye.
ipe nunapa kiakampi naisikkaliye.
ipe nunapa kiakampi tuypulamakkaliye.
inna ipekantinaye.   420
tuu sopa.

inna ipekantinaye.
palimakkialimalainiye.

inna ipekan walepunkanaye.
ipe kwakwalikampi naisikkaliye.   425
ipe kwakwalikampi tuypulamakkaliye.
tuu pina kannoaliye.
tuu pina machoaliye.

inna ipekan walepunkanaye.
ipe kikkaki pakkwamakkakine.   430
akku kal alulumakkaliye.
akku kala tonimakkaliye.
tuu pina kannoali.
tuu pina machoaliye.

inna ipekan walepunkanaye.   435
ipe pipyaki tulekineye.
wakal alulumakkekwichiye.
wakala kinnoekwichiye.
tuu pina kannoekwichi.
tuu pina machoekwichiye.   440

tuu sopa yaiti kaoppoli walapi kaekwichiye.
tuu sopa yaiti machi inna ittoappileleti.
kaoppoli walati kaekwichiye.

tuu sopa yaitinaye.
tuu sop e posumpa nekaki pup aipiryekwichiye.   445
pupa na aipiliali.
e posumpa yapi tarpa noekwichiye.
ipe korikka sailakampi neka pilli tulote.
tuu kuna nekaseye.

They are getting fortified for the libation.   415
They are getting valiant for the libation.

The spouses of the owners of chicha.
They are hanging on their sacred *nunap* (sweet smelling native plant)
    beads.
They are putting on bunches of sacred *nunap* beads.
And the owners of chicha.   420
The libation maker.

And the owners of chicha.
They are announcing.

The spouses of the owners of chicha.
They are hanging on sacred bead necklaces.   425
They are putting on bunches of sacred bead necklaces.
They are getting fortified for the libation.
They are getting valiant for the libation.

The spouses of the owners of chicha.
With sacred *makep* (red dye).   430
They are coloring their cheeks pink.
They are making designs on their cheeks.
They are getting fortified for the libation.
They are getting valiant for the libation.

The spouses of the owners of chicha.   435
With sacred mirrors.
They are standing coloring their cheeks pink.
They are standing reddening their faces.
They are standing fortifying themselves for the libation.
They are standing being valiant for the libation.   440

The libation maker is standing holding his staff.
The chicha tasting boys of the libation maker.
Are standing holding their staffs.

And the libation maker.
The libation maker is standing twirling himself about in his abode his
    house.   445
He is twirling himself about.
He is standing going out of the portal of his abode.
He fills the place with the sound of the chiefs of the sacred pelican (type
    of flute made from pelican bone).
Toward the chicha place the house.

tuu sopa yaitinaye.   450
ipe tetepana sailakampi neka pilli tuloteye.
neka pilli waytikkoteye.

ee sopa yaitinaye.
ipe korikka sailakampi neka pilli tuloteye.
neka pilli waytikkote.   455
tuu kuna posumpa iwala paliye.

ena ipekantinaye.
ipe kala pipila walakampi neka pilli tuloteye.
neka pilli waytikkoteye.
tuu kuna posumpa iwala paliye.   460

pupa wal ituamayteye.
pupa wala muchuppimayteye.
tuu kuna posumpa nekasekaye.

tuu kunaye posumpa nekasekaye.
olo kanaye maisu ina pilli ukakka paliye.   465
pupa na marwitappiye.
tuu kun nekasekaye.

inna pomettekampi yallemakkesii.
inna pomettenakampi inikkimakkaliye.
inna pomettenakampi yallemaysattikineye.   470

tuu sopa yaiti, pupa naikusale.
neka pillipi pali soytapinneye.
tuu sopa yai, e walepunkwa, na palimakkiali.
olo kana maisu ina pilli ukakka pali.
pupa na sermechaliye.   475
pupa na ituamakkaliye.

tuu sopa yaiti kwekitup otimakkesikwisa, neka pillipi pali sokkaliye.
neka pillipi pali sokesiiye.
tuu sopa yai, e walepunkwa, tuu sopa yaise pupa kwichikunikkiye.

"na pey olo kurkinate suetanikkisummawa."   480
tuu sopa yai na palimakkiali, e walepunkwaseka.
"olo kurkinate peka ukketisuliwa."

And the libation maker.   450
He fills the place with the sound of the chiefs of the sacred armadillo
    (type of flute made from armadillo and bird bones).
He fills the place with their noise.

And the maker of it.
He fills the place with the sound of the chiefs of the sacred pelican.
He fills the place with their noise.   455
Along the way to the libation place the abode.

And the owners of the drink.
They fill the place with the sound of the sacred whistling bones (flutes).
They fill the place with noise.
Along the way to the libation place the abode.   460

They step themselves along.
They move themselves back and forth.
Toward the libation place the abode the house.

Toward the libation place the abode the house.
Up to the golden bench the sacred side one.   465
They went and sat themselves down there.
Toward the libation place the house.

The chicha vessels are being placed in order according to strength.
The chicha vessels are being lined up according to strength.
The chicha vessels have been put in order according to strength.   470

The libation maker, feels himself inebriated.
He already fills the place with talk again.
The spouse, of the libation maker, is now announcing.
Up to the long golden bench the sacred side one again.
She is drifting herself along.   475
She is stepping herself along.

The libation maker was sitting gathering heart, he is filling the place with
    talk again.
He is sitting filling the place with talk again.
The spouse, of the libation maker, went to stand herself in front of the
    libation maker.

"Now I have come to take away your golden hat."   480
The libation maker is now announcing, to his spouse.
"I do not give you the golden hat."

tuu sopa yai e walepunkwa na palimakkiali.
"ei olo korpattanakampi esikkesummawa."
olo korpattanakampi pal esikkekwichiye.   485

"tuu sopa yaitina pe pali wisikutosuliye.
anti tuu pakkana penekuesimoiniye.
tuu pakkana ante wimakkena soke simoiniye."

pupa wala ituamayteye.
pupa wala muchuppimayteye.   490
olo kana maisu ina pilli ukakka paliye.
tuu sopa yai e walepunkwa pupa na marwitappiye.

tuu sopa yai na palimakkialiye.
ipe narsopa pilli yala paliye.
inna ipekantinaye, ipe ilala walatikampi, pioylealiye.   495
tuu sopa yai neka palitakkesikwisa, tuu kuna nekakineye.

ipe narsopa pilli yala paliye.
ipe tole tole wisimalattiye.
tuu pomette naka paliye.
pupa na mesekwichiye.   500
ipekana suitakke tulekanaye.
tuu kuna posumpa nekakineye.

inna ipekantinaye, uu karpa ipe narsopa, pilli yala paliye.
uu karpa totokkwakankineye.
ipe sikkilakampi ampakualiye.   505
tuu kuna nekakineye.
tuu sopa yaiti neka palitakkesikwisaye.

tuu sopa, ipe narsopa pilli yala pali, uu karpa totokkwakankine.
ipe nirpakkikampi, ulusikwialiye.
tuu sopa yaiti neka palitakkesikwisaye.   510
tuu kuna nekakineye.

ipe narsopa pilli yala paliye.
ipe muttula walakampi, uu karpa totokkwakanki mekwialiye.
tuu sopa yaiti, neka palitakkesikwisaye.
tuu kuna nekakineye.   515

The spouse, of the libation maker is now announcing.
"I will take only your golden tie(s)."
He is standing taking off his golden tie(s) only.   485

"Libation maker I will not know you again.
I also compete with the libation (drink chicha).
I will go and sweat (am ready to taste) the libation I say I will."

She steps herself along.
She moves herself back and forth.   490
Up to the golden bench the sacred one again.
The spouse of the libation maker went there and now sat herself down.

The libation maker is now announcing (giving instructions).
On top of the sacred balsa wood.
The owners of chicha, are nailing palm, wood shelves.   495
The libation maker was sitting watching over this, within the libation
    place the house.

On top of the sacred balsa wood.
The knowers (caretakers) of the sacred *tole tole* (flutes of the *kantule*,
    master of ceremonies of girls' puberty rites).
Beside the libation vessels.
They placed them themselves (the flutes).   500
The caretaker people.
Within the libation place the abode the house.

The owners of chicha, (place) an *uu* basket on top of, the sacred balsa
    wood.
A tiny *uu* basket.
They are placing sacred *sikki* (small pointed) cups (inside the basket). 505
Within the libation place the house.
The libation maker was sitting watching over this.

The libation maker, on top of the sacred balsa wood, inside the tiny *uu*
    basket.
They (the owners of chicha) are placing, the sacred cotton.
The libation maker was sitting watching over this.   510
Within the libation place the house.

On top of the sacred balsa wood.
They are placing the sacred resin, in the tiny *uu* basket.
The libation maker, was sitting watching over this.
Within the libation place the house.   515

tuu sopa yaitinaye.
ipe narsopa pilli yala paliye.
ipe siysikkwakampi naisikkalimalaye.
ipe narsopa pilli yala paliye.
tuu sopa yaiti neka palitakkesikwisaye.   520
tuu kuna nekakineye.

ipe narsopa pilli yala paliye.
ipe akkela walakampiye, naisikkalimala.
inna ipekantinaye.
tuu sopa yaiti neka palitakkesikwisaye.   525

ipe narsopa pilli yala paliye.
ipe akkela walakampi naisiytemalattikineye.
olo kachi tupakampi pilealiye.
tuu sopa yai.
neka palitakkesikwisaye.   530

ipe narsopaye pilli yala paliye.
ipe akkelawalakampi ampakualiye.
ipe ti nokakampi ampakualiye.
ipe nirpakkikampi pilealiye.
tuu sopa yai, neka palitakkesikwisaye.   535
tuu kuna nekakineye.

ipe narsopa pilli yala paliye.
ipe korikka nokakampi, ampakualiye.
ipe korikka nokakampi, ilemakke nasaa.
tuu sopa yai, neka palitakkesii.   540
tuu kuna nekakineye.

ipe narsopa pilli yala paliye.
ipe korikka nokakampi palekinyesiiye.
palekinyamakkesiiye.
tuuye, tuu kuna nekapi palitakkesiiye.   545
tuu sopa yaitinaye.

ipe narsopa pilli yala paliye.
salu punnu kurkinapiye.
sikwialiye.
tuu sopa yai, neka palitakkesikwisa.   550
tuu kuna nekakineye.

ipe narsopaye na pilli yala paliye.
ipe salu punnu kurkinapi palekinyesiiye.

And the libation maker.
On top of the sacred balsa wood.
They (the owners of chicha) are hanging the sacred rattle.
On top of the sacred balsa wood.
The libation maker was sitting watching over this. 520
Within the libation place the house.

On top of the sacred balsa wood.
They are hanging, the sacred (wooden hammock for the *kantule*) hooks.
And the owners of chicha.
The libation maker was sitting watching over this. 525

On top of the sacred balsa wood.
When they have hung the sacred hooks.
They are attaching the golden hammock ropes.
The libation maker.
Was sitting watching over this. 530

On top of the sacred balsa wood.
They are placing on the sacred hooks.
They are placing the sacred water cups (for mouth rinsing).
They are attaching them with sacred cotton.
The libation maker, was sitting watching over this. 535
Within the libation place the house.

On top of the sacred balsa wood.
They are placing, the sacred pelican (shaped) cups.
They are lining up, the sacred pelican (shaped) cups.
The libation maker, is sitting watching over this. 540
Within the libation place the house.

On top of the sacred balsa wood.
The sacred cups are sitting appearing like sacred pelicans.
They are sitting appearing.
The libation, in the very libation place the house he is sitting watching
    over this. 545
The libation maker he is.

On top of the sacred balsa wood.
The very macaw feather hat (*kantule's* hat).
They are placing.
The libation maker, was sitting watching over this. 550
Within the libation place the house.

On top of the sacred balsa wood.
The very hat is sitting appearing like the sacred macaw feather.

ipe salu punnu kurkinapi, ailewamakkesiiye.
tuu sopa yai, neka palitakkesikwisaye.   555
tuu kuna nekakineye.

tuu sopa yaiti neka palitakkesiiye.
tuu kuna nekakineye.
tole tole wisimalattiye.
pupa wala na aipannaliye.   560
pupa wala na ituamakkaliye.
tuu kuna nekasekaye.

tuu sopa yaiti, neka palitakkesiiye.
tuu kuna nekakineye.
ipekana suitakke tulekanaye.   565
pupa na aipannaliye.
pupa wal ituamakkaliye.
tuu kuna nekasekaye.

tuu sopa yai neka palitakkesiiye.
ipe naye.   570
ipe nala takke tulekanaye.
pupa wal aipannaliye.
pupa wal ituamakkaliye.
tuu kuna nekasekaye.

tuu sopa yaiti, neka palitakkesiiye.   575
ipe noka takke tulekanaye.
pupa na aipannaliye.
pupa wala ituamakkaliye.
tuu kuna nekasekaye.

tuu sopa yai neka palitakkesiiye.   580
ipe kaspak sae tulekanaye.
pupa wal aipannaliye.
pupa wala selealialiye.
pupa wala muchuppimakkaliye.
tuu kuna nekasekaye.   585

tuu sopa yai neka palitakkesiiye.
tuu sopa yai neka palitakkesiiye.
e ie tulekanaye pupa na aipannaliye.
pupa wala ituamakkali.
pupa wala muchuppimakkaliye.   590
tuu kuna nekasekaye.

The sacred macaw feather hat, is sitting waving from side to side.
The libation maker, was sitting watching over this.   *555*
Within the libation place the house.

The libation maker is sitting watching over this.
Within the libation place the house.
Those who know the *tole tole* (*kantules*).
They are swaying themselves along.   *560*
They are now stepping themselves along.
Toward the libation place the house.

The libation maker, is sitting watching over this.
Within the libation place the house.
The caretaker people (ritual officials).   *565*
They are swaying themselves along.
They are stepping themselves along.
Toward the libation place the house.

The libation maker is sitting watching over this.
The sacred incense burner.   *570*
The sacred incense burner caretaker people (ritual officials).
They are swaying themselves along.
They are stepping themselves along.
Toward the libation place the house.

The libation maker, is sitting watching over this.   *575*
The sacred cup caretaker people (ritual officials).
They are now swaying themselves along.
They are stepping themselves along.
Toward the libation place the house.

The libation maker is sitting watching over this.   *580*
The sacred hammock rope maker people (ritual officials).
They are swaying themselves along.
They are drifting themselves along.
They are moving themselves back and forth.
Toward the libation place the house.   *585*

The libation maker is sitting watching over this.
The libation maker is sitting watching over this.
The ritual haircutter people (women who ritually cut pubescent girls'
    hair) are now swaying themselves along.
They are stepping themselves along.
They are moving themselves back and forth.   *590*
Toward the libation place the house.

ti kae tule kanaye, pupa wal aipannaliye.
pupa wal ituamakkali.
pupa wala muchuppimakkali.
tuu kuna nekasekaye.   595

tole tole wisimalattiye.
kala pipila walakan imayteye.
unni ukakka pal ittokelesuliye.

ipe korikka sailakan imayteye.
unni ukakka pal ittokelesuliye.   600

tetepa sailakampi neka pilli tulote.
neka pillikampi waitikkoteye.
unni ukakka pal ittokelesuliye.
tuu sopa yaiti neka palitakkesiiye.
tuu kuna nekakineye.   605

tuu sopa yaiti neka palitakkesiiye.
inna ipekan walepunkan imayte.
olo sakkila wal imayteye.
olo sakkila turpakwal imayteye.
unni ukakka pal ittokelesuliye.   610
tuu sopa yai neka palitakkesiiye.
tuu kuna nekakineye.

walepunkan imayteye.
unni ukakka pal ittokelesuliye.
inna ipekan imayteye.   615
unni ukakka pal ittokelesuliye.

tuu sopa yaitinaye, pupa nai kusale.
tuu kuna posumpa nekaki, aitikesiiye.
inna pomettekampi yallemaysattikineye.
inna pomettekampi inikkimaysattikineye.   620

tuu sopa yaitinaye.
kweki tup otimakkesiiye.
"kepe ilakwen takkeye," kep ipi sokewa.
"ante kusaku inna ipekanka saettinaye."
tuu sopa yaitina, palimayyesiiye.   625

The ritual water carrying people (ritual officials), are swaying themselves
    along.
They are stepping themselves along.
They are moving themselves back and forth.
Toward the libation place the house.   595

Those who know *tole tole*.
Sound out the whistling bones (small flutes made from animal bones).
Their different tones cannot be distinguished.

They sound out the sacred pelican chiefs (flutes made from pelican
    bones).
Their different tones cannot be distinguished.   600

They sound out the sacred armadillo chiefs (flutes made from armadillo
    skull).
They fill the place with noise.
Their different tones cannot be distinguished.
The libation maker is sitting watching over this.
Within the libation place the house.   605

The libation maker is sitting watching over this.
The spouses of the owners of chicha sound out.
The golden necklaces sound out.
Their golden seeded necklaces sound out.
Their different tones cannot be distinguished.   610
The libation maker is sitting watching over this.
Within the libation place the house.

The spouses sound out.
Their different tones cannot be distinguished
The owners of chicha sound out.   615
Their different tones cannot be distinguished.

And the libation maker, he feels himself inebriated.
He is sitting, within his place the abode the house.
Having put the chicha vessels in order.
Having lined up the chicha vessels.   620

And the libation maker.
He is sitting gathering heart.
"This is not the first time," is what he says.
"I have done this before for the owners of chicha."
And the libation maker, he is sitting announcing.   625

inna ipekanti imayteye.
ipe korikka nokakampiye.
imayteye, neka pillikampi tuloteye.
neka pillikampi koormayteye.
unni ukakka pal ittokelesuliye.   630

inna ipekan imayteye.
tuupi ittokekwikwichiye.
inna ipekantinaye.
tuupi pal ittokeyolaye.
inna ipekan imayteye.   635

inna ipekan imayteye.
"weki na wisikuele kepe suliwaye."
inna ipekan imayteye.

inna ipekana imayteye.
unni ukakka pal ittokelesuliye.   640
inna ipekan imayteye.

inna ipekanti tuu tiki naikusaleye.
inna ipekanti imayteye.

inna ipekantinaye.
olo kansu pillikan, akkimakkaliye.   645
olo kansu pillikan aitalialiye.
tuu sopa yaiti neka palitakkesiiye.
tuu kuna nekakineye.

olo kansu pillikanti karkaloaliye.
tuu sopa yaiti neka palitakkesiiye.   650
tuu kuna nekakineye.

inna ipekanti pal ainakkwemaiye.
uu kachiki pal ainakkwemai.
muchuppi pal aitemaiye.
inna tuu sopa yait neka palitakkesiiye.   655
tuu kuna nekakineye.

The owners of chicha sound out.
The very sacred pelican shaped cups.
They sound out, they fill the place with sound.
They fill the place with shouting.
Their different tones cannot be distinguished.   630

The owners of chicha sound out.
They are standing tasting the very libation.
And the owners of chicha.
They are tasting again the very libation.
The owners of chicha sound out.   635

The owners of chicha sound out.
"This is the way we want to be."
The owners of chicha sound out.

The owners of chicha sound out.
Their different tones cannot be distinguished.   640
The owners of chicha sound out.

The owners of chicha feel inebriated with the libation.
The owners of chicha sound out.

And the owners of chicha.
They are emptying, the long golden side benches.   645
They are scattering the long golden side benches.
The libation maker is sitting watching over this.
Within the libation place the house.

The long golden side benches are being thrown about.
The libation maker is sitting watching over this.   650
Within the libation place the house.

The owners of chicha are again lying down.
They are again lying in the sacred hammocks.
One after the other they are lying down.
The libation maker is sitting watching over this.   655
Within the libation place the house.

Figure 17. Machi Esakunappi on the beach watching his wives in the sea

Chapter 10

The Way of the Sea Turtle

Performed by Tiowilikinya

Yaukka ikar/The Way of the Sea Turtle was performed by Tiowilikinya
in his home in Mulatuppu in March 1979. Tiowilikinya was a medicinal specialist who could be seen every day carrying on long poles on his
shoulders large quantities of medicine he had gathered in the jungle. He
was a tall and strong man, strikingly dark in complexion for a Kuna. He
had a good sense of humor and in addition to his knowledge of Kuna
medicine, he knew several chants that are performed during puberty rites
for young girls, for the pleasure of a gathered audience, as well as representatives of the spirit world who listen in. *The Way of the Sea Turtle* is
one of these.

The performance of *The Way of the Sea Turtle*, like other chants that
the Kuna call "play ways," as well as serious magical and curing chants,
is one of the many activities that occur during young girls' puberty rites
and festivities. In addition to official ritual events such as the cutting of
the hair of the young girl, the chanting of the *kantule* (master of ceremonies of the event), ceremonial dancing, and ritual and not so ritual drinking, many other activities take place. These include playing panpipes,
arguing, endless joking, attempts at speaking various languages, and making fun of others.[1] And people who know chants such as *The Way of the
Sea Turtle* are expected to perform them spontaneously, even though they
are not an official part of the ritual. Performance is also common at home
at night, before falling asleep. The performer lies in his hammock and
chants, while family members, spirits, and, in this case, I, listen in. I know
of two other versions of *The Way of the Sea Turtle*, neither one available in recorded form, as far as I know.[2]

While it contains playful and humorous elements, *The Way of the Sea
Turtle* is a serious story that can be interpreted as offering several messages. Interestingly, this chant, which is performed at girls' puberty rites,

chicha festivals, ends, in a climactic moment, with a description of a chicha festival. In general terms, it is the story of a man who loses his wife to a sea turtle who carries her away, and then recovers her in the afterworld after his own death. The story consists of the following episodes.

1. A man, Machi Esakunappi, and his several wives come upon a sea turtle about to lay eggs on the beach and compete in trying to turn her over (lines 1–14).

2. The women get stuck to the turtle and get carried away on the waves (lines 15–34).

3. Machi Esakunappi is at home alone after losing his wives. While he is at first sad, little by little he forgets them and resumes his life (lines 35–40).

4. Machi Esakunappi is killed by an evil spirit, Devil, and, like his wives, is taken away (lines 41–49).

5. Machi Esakunappi goes on the sea with Devil and a whole flotilla of boats belonging to evil spirits, all headed to Devil's home, his stronghold, where Machi Esakunappi will be given a new wife (lines 50–121).

6. At Devil's stronghold a puberty rites festival is taking place. Machi Esakunappi refuses all the women offered to him by Devil and discovers his own lost wife and wants to marry her. There is a drinking competition, which Machi Esakunappi wins and as a result obtains the wife he wants (line 122–193).

GRAMMAR, STYLE, VOCABULARY

The Way of the Sea Turtle is addressed to representatives of the spirit world and shares grammatical and stylistic features with curing and magical chants. From a grammatical perspective this involves most strikingly the use of longer and fuller forms than in everyday speech; the use of verbal suffixes that indicate with incredible precision the position, movement, direction, and timing of the action involved; and the very frequent use of the suffix *-ye* in line final position.

The use of linear parallelism is an important aspect of the poetry of *The Way of the Sea Turtle*. There are many parallel lines in this text. The descriptions of the fleet of evil spirits on the sea, in sets of parallel lines and phrases, and of their wives coming to the dock to wait for them, are very striking.

> Sacred Uncle Shark's silver boat is coming into sight, Sacred
> Uncle Devilfish's silver boat is coming into sight.

Sacred Uncle Devil's boats zigzag past each other.
The boats dance along on the waves.
They circle along on the waves.

All Sacred Devilfish's spouses are descending.
All Sacred Uncle Shark's spouses are descending.

Certain lines are repeated throughout the text, with slight variations:

Machi Esakunappi is standing watching this.

Machi Esakunappi is sitting gathering heart.

Quoted dialogues, rather than third person descriptions by the narrator, are characteristic of all Kuna discourse. They are frequent in this performance of *The Way of the Sea Turtle*. The climactic ending in particular is expressed through a series of quoted dialogues.

The vocabulary of *The Way of the Sea Turtle* is esoteric, metaphorical, and playful. It provides a poetic imagination and a magical realism to this text. Examples of esoteric words, some of which are found in other texts in this book, are *walepunkwa* for "wife," which I translate as "spouse"; *posumpa* or *kalu* for "house/home," which I translate as "abode" and "stronghold"; and *kalu pilli* for "outer walls of house," which I translate as "towers." "To gather heart" is used as a metaphor for "think." I translate "eye liquid" as sobbing. An interesting expression used in this chant is *muu kunwa*, literally, the "sea's lightning bugs." *Muu* is an esoteric word for sea, which has many ritual denotations and connotations, including grandmother, midwife, and birth, as well as sea. The expression *muu kunwa* is used here to describe poetically the playful, sparkling, dancing light and movement of the waves, and I translate it as "sparklings of the waves."

Human kinship terms are used in *The Way of the Sea Turtle* for animals and spirits, "aunt niece," a strange combination of two terms, for the sea turtle, and "uncle" for Devil and evil animal spirits. This use of kin terms is an expression of the close relationship between the worlds of humans, animals, and spirits in the Kuna belief system as well as a source of humor. The major human protagonists in the story have traditional, ritual Kuna names, Machi Esakunappi for the husband and Sister Golden Makkili Sopikwaye for the wife. *Machi* means boy or son; both Machi and Puna "Sister" are frequently used in traditional Kuna names. While these are ritual names, in the context of this chant they are somewhat humorous as well. Machi in particular, especially when used alone, as it is in several instances, precisely because it means a boy, not yet a mature man, has humorous connotations. A good example is the arrival of Machi Esakunappi to the stronghold of Devil, where he is met by Devil's wives, who proclaim

> "New people have come it seems.
> Sacred Uncle Devil came and lowered (brought) a new *machi* it seems."

Certain elements in this text require explanation for a non Kuna audience. Sea turtles are remarkable animals that travel widely throughout the Caribbean region.[3] This story reflects their incredible traveling ability and the Kuna perception and imagination of it. Sea turtles have played an important role in the Kuna diet and economy. The Kuna eat their meat and eggs and sell their shells to foreigners. Unfortunately, sea turtles, like the Kuna literature represented here, are in danger of extinction, a tragic case of a relationship between language and ecology.

As expressed in this chant, the sea that surrounds most Kuna villages is both a place of beauty and bounty and a source of evil. It contains fish and other animals important in the Kuna diet and mythology. But it also harbors creatures and evil spirits that can cause great harm. The Kuna are seafaring people who feel quite comfortable on and indeed love the water. At the same time they fear the dangers the sea might hold for them.

The Kuna believe, as do many people, that after death one enters another world. Here we are offered a glimpse of the Kuna afterworld. For those who merit it, it is a world of strongholds and towers, gold and silver, wealth and happiness.

It seems that Machi Esakunappi has several wives, though it is his principal wife, Sister Golden Makkili Sopikwaye, whom he encounters at the end of the story. Kuna men probably used to have more than one wife, a practice highly unusual and frowned on today. In this text, while providing a glimpse of the past, it is also a source of humor.

More generally, this story, like several others in this book, reflects and comments on Kuna sexual relations and preferences, and issues of gender in Kuna society. First, there is sexual innuendo. The Kuna associate sea turtles with sex, and both men and women joke about this quite overtly, explicitly, and boisterously. When a male turtle is caught, people touch and talk about his sexual parts. Female turtles lay their eggs on the beach, and this provides an opportunity for the Kuna to catch them, or to play with them, as in this story. It is believed that sea turtles are sticky, and the sea turtle in this story uses this characteristic to snatch away Machi Esakunappi's wife. There is clearly a hint that Machi Esakunappi's wives are having sexual relations with the turtles. Both husband and wife are tempted by and invited to attach themselves to other partners, but in the end return to each other.

This leads to the question of what the message or moral of *The Way of the Sea Turtle* is. It seems as though there are several and these are related. Husbands should be loyal to their wives and wives to their husbands. Perhaps both should be monogamous, but there is a certain ambiguity and humor here. While it is tempting to marry outside one's ethnic group, in the end, one should stick to one's own kind. This is the meaning of Machi Esakunappi not wanting to marry women with flat noses. The Kuna ethnic aesthetic favors long noses.

This story, like other texts in this book, expresses the importance of chicha rites and festivities, both in the past and in the present. Among many other activities, chicha festivities are the site of couples meeting, drinking together, and competing, often leading to marriage.

Olokwagdi de Akwanusadup's illustration for *The Way of the Sea Turtle* shows Machi Esakunappi standing on the beach as his wives walk out into the sea (fig. 17). One can clearly see the sparklings of the waves. There are plants and trees and a clump of mangroves in the landscape. The sea is both attractive and dangerous, with waves that get higher and higher in the distance. A shadowy figure seated on a canoe (probably Devil) is watching Machi Esakunappi. Machi Esakunappi and shadowy Devil are wearing what Olokwagdi imagines Kuna men traditionally to have worn, and his wives are in the contemporary dress of Kuna women.

My photograph shows Tiowilikinya, standing in his house, beside a medicine basket he has not yet finished making (photo 23).

The chant, which begins with *waiye*, indicating that it is addressed to the spirit world, is typically Kuna—a mix of serious and playful, moralistic and humorous. Here is *The Way of the Sea Turtle*, as performed by Tiowilikinya.

Kuna

waiye.
machi olo machiti, machi esakunappiye sunnamakkeye.
na walepunkanaka sunnamakkekwichiye.

"muu kunwa nanati na peka takkenaye.

muu kunwa nanati na peka takkenae, wiluppise walamaysa ittoleye."
machi esakunappiye na walepunkanka sunnamakkekwichiye.　　　　　5

machi esakunappiye tinaye, amma sia pali takkekwichiye.
muu pillisikkiye, amma sia nik kolekwichiye.

na walepunkwa yalapa aipiryekwichiye muu pillipali amma sia nikka tar
　　kolekwichiye.

amma siatinaye, muu pillipa nakkwetanikkiye.
machi esakunappiye neka pali takkekwichiye.　　　　　　　　　　10

na walepunkanaye, machi esakunappiye ka sunnamakkekwichikwaye.
"na wis ittomokoerkeye, pule kalanikkatipaye, pe ittoele kepe
　　pittosuliwaliye."
machi esakunappiye na walepunkanka sunnamakkekwichiye.

walepunkanaye amma sia, epuekwichiye.
amma siatiki allilite takkekwichi machi esakunappiye esakunappi.　　15
machi esakunnapiye kwaketup otimakkekwichi "papakante par ittosa
　　ittoleye melle omese achaoeye" ome sakkwa wala oyoenai muu
　　pillipali.
muu pillipa aitekema amma siatinaye.

machi esakunappiye muu pillipa pali takkekwichiye.
muu pilliki arkwatte walepunkana tar pali takkekwichiye.

muu pilli ukakkaki, walepunkan naikutappi amma sia naikutappiye.　20
naye machi esakunappiye walepunkana tar takkekwichikusaye.

English

waiye.
Machi the golden *machi*, Machi Esakunappi speaks.
Now he is standing speaking to his spouses.

"I am now showing you Mother of the Sparklings of the Waves (the sea
  turtle's ritual playname).

Let us go now and see Mother of the Sparklings of the Waves, the
  moment to do it has arrived it seems (the turtle is about to lay her eggs
  on the beach)."
Machi Esakunappiye is now standing speaking to his spouses.   5

And Machi Esakunappi, is now standing watching Aunt Niece (another
  ritual name of the sea turtle).
Toward the waves, he is standing calling directly to Aunt Niece.

Now beside his spouse he is twirling about toward the waves he is
  standing calling directly to Aunt Niece.

And Aunt Niece, comes and rises on the waves.
Machi Esakunappi is standing watching this.   10

Now the spouses, Machi Esakunappi is standing speaking to them.
"Now let us find out, how strong she is (by turning her over), first you
  will try don't you hear."
Machi Esakunappi is now standing speaking to his spouses.

The spouses are standing touching, Aunt Niece.
They get stuck to Aunt Niece Machi Esakunappi is standing seeing this
  Esakunappi is.   15
Machi Esakunappi is standing gathering heart (thinking) "This is one of
  those (sticky turtles) the elders listen (chant) about (in the gathering
  house) do not touch the woman" the woman is raising her arm on the
  waves.
And Aunt Niece is descending on the waves.

Machi Esakunappi is standing watching the waves.
He is standing watching the spouses fall in the waves.

Out on the waves, the spouses are floating there Aunt Niece is floating
  there.   20
Now Machi Esakunappi was standing seeing the spouses.

"na pe mette naeye," machi esakunappiye se walepunkana
sunnamakkekwichiye.
kalakwensuli ome sunnamakkenai, muu pillipali "nele niakkwa nele pe
pillipa pe otukkusamokana yerpanaye.
na mette muu pillipa nae" sokenaikuaye.

amma siati muu pillikalapaliye.   25
walepunkanaka ipe kopukka wala toyteye.
muu pillipa aiteteye.
machi esakunappiye tar pali takkekwichiye.

pali tar pali taysasuliye.
amma sia oetete.   30
machi esakunappiye neka pali takkekwichiye.

"na walepunkanati amma sia pakka tar ani nekati ipekunate" an
takkeye.
machi esakunappiye tar kwaketup otimakkekwichi solapaliye.

tatamala apalakusa olo tatamala apalakusa machi esakunappiye nekase
aipilisaye.
waiye waiye.

"na walepunkana unni ielekesuliye," kwekitupa tala nisa apalaki machi
esakunappiye.   35
aipirresikwisaye.

ipakuna paapakkakineye.
walepunkana ieali.
muu yalapillipaliye yalapillipali.
ipi tulakala amienaesokkaliye, machi esakunappiye, ipe kupettuwala
kakakwichikusaye.   40

yalapillipaliye, kilu niakkwa neleye, na apikuekwichikusaye.
kilu niakkwa nele nekati ipekuteye machi esakunappiyeti.
sana tar oeletemokarkeye.

neka par ittosasuli machi esakunappiye aitikemekwisaye.
kilu niakkwa nelekanpa neka ipekute.   45
kalu tummakampa nekakwa ipekuteye.

na walepunkana pali wisikusasuli.
machi esakunappiyeti kilu niakkwa nele ulukka ealite.
ulukka oeletemokarkeye.

"Now we are leaving you," the spouses are standing saying to Machi
  Esakunappi.
The woman is saying all different kinds of things, on the waves "I would
  have preferred that Sacred Devil hide you at his stronghold.
I am leaving you on the waves I am going" she is saying as she goes
  along.

Aunt Niece is on her way on the waves.   25
The *kopukka* wood coconut trees are passing the spouses by (for the
  last time).
They descend on the waves.
Machi Esakunapii is standing watching.

Then he did not see any more.
Aunt niece disappeared.   30
Machi Esakunappiye is standing watching this.

"Now the spouses will dwell together with Aunt Niece" I see.
Machi Esakunappi is standing gathering heart afterwards.

When the sun was at its halfway point when the golden sun was at its
  halfway point Machi Esakunappi returned home.
waiye waiye.

"The spouses will never be forgotten," Machi Esakunappi's heart was
  in the middle of the flowing of his sobbings.   35
He was sitting twirling around.

After eight days.
He begins to forget the spouses.
(He went) to the mountain peaks to the mountain.
Machi Esakunappi, is about to go and hunt animals, he was standing
  holding his sacred armament.   40

In the mountain, he was now standing encountering, Sacred Uncle Devil.
Machi Esakunappi dwells with Sacred Uncle Devil.
He too (like his wife) disappears.

Machi Esakunappi no longer felt life he lay on the ground.
He dwells together with Sacred Uncle Devils.   45
He dwells at their big stronghold.

Now he no longer remembered his spouses.
And Sacred Uncle Devil takes away Machi Esakunappi's skin (life).
His skin disappears also.

ipakalakwin tulakwenattikineye.   50
kilu niakkwa nele.
machi esakunappi eka tar naesokkaliye.
muukwa tar pillipaliye.

kilu niakkwa nele nitesokkali machi esakunappiye.
esa mani uluki onakkwialiye.   55

kiluye sunnamakkekwichiye machi esakunappiye ka sunnamakkaliye.
"muu tar makattipa na pe nitekuerkeye.
ani walepunkana na peka uytappoeye."

man esa uluki nakkwisa machi esakunappiyeti.
kilu niakkwa nele ulu.   60
ka sermesemekwisaye tar muukwa tar pillipaliye.

kilu nele man esa ulu tar pukkipa tar ainimaiye.
machi esakunappiye neka tar pali taynatappiye.

machi esakunappiye, kilu niakkwa nele, uluyaki kwekitup otimakkesii.
"walepunkanase walepunkana kachi tupa nasiysamalattiye.   65
kannalase pali aipirye nae kepe pali" ipi sokekuarkeye.

"kilu nele niakkwa nelepa nekati ipkuna taylesunye."
machi esakunappiye tar sunna kwaketup otimakkesi.
kilu niakkwa uluyakineye.

kilu ulu pulekan ainimaiye.   70
machi esakunappiye neka tar pali taysiye, muu pillipa.
kilu niakkwa nele ulu tar kinnemekwisaye.

kilu niakkwa nele man esa ulu totonatappi muu pillipaliye.
muu pillikana iirmakkemaikwaye.
machi neka tar pali taynatappiye.   75

machi tar kwekitup otimayye.
"nana sailati kannala kalu poosumpase nana sailati pali takkenaeye,"
   kepe ipi sokekuaye.

machi esakunappiye tar kwekitup otimaysiye, tala nis apalakineye, kilu
   niakkwa nele.
man esa ulu yakineye.

Within twenty days.   50
With Sacred Uncle Devil.
Machi Esakunappi is about to go.
On the waves.

Sacred Uncle Devil is about to carry Machi Esakunappi away.
Within his silver boat he is raising him.   55

Uncle is standing speaking he is speaking to Machi Esakunappi.
"I will carry you far away on the waves.
I will give you spouses there."

Into the silver boat Machi Esakunappi climbed.
Sacred Uncle Devil's boat.   60
They stood drifting off over the waves.

Sacred Uncle's many boats are coming into sight.
Machi Esakunappiye watches this as he goes along.

Machi Esakunappiye, within Sacred Uncle Devil's, boat is sitting
    gathering heart.
"When I strung up the hammock for the spouses the spouses (in order
    to sleep with them).   65
You (Machi Esakunappiye) will not turn back to that (do that again)"
    is what he said.

"I will dwell at Sacred Uncle Devil the Sacred One's place it seems."
Machi Esakunappiye is truly sitting gathering heart.
Within Uncle Devil's boat.

Uncle's valiant army of boats is coming into sight.   70
Machi Esakunappiye is sitting watching this, on the waves.
Sacred Uncle Devil's boat was speeding along.

Sacred Uncle Devil's silver boat dances along on the waves.
The waves are fluttering by.
Machi watches this as he goes along.   75

Machi gathers heart.
"My mother's place of origin I will never again go and see my mother's
    stronghold her abode my mother's place of origin," is what he says.

Machi Esakunappi is sitting gathering heart, in the middle of the flowing
    of his sobbings, within.
Sacred Uncle Devil's silver boat.

machi esakunappiye neka taynatappikwaye.   80
kilu nalikka nele man esa ulu ainimaiye, kilu nitarpaki nele man esa
   ulu ainimaiye.

kilu niakkwa nele ulupa muchumakke yolaki.
man esa ulukanti tar muu pillipa totonatappiye.
muu pillipa piryamakkenatappiye.
machi neka tar pali taynatappiye.   85

machi esakunappiye neka taynatappikwaye.
ulu tar pukkipa ainimaiye.
kilu tar makatti tola ulu ainimaiye.

muu pillipa ulu totonatappikwaye.
muu pillipa ulu nakkwamakkenatappikwaye.   90
muu pillikan tar kwichikumaikwaye.
machi neka tar pali taynatappiye.

muu pillikana iirmakkemaikwaye.
muu pillikana man esa ulu tarpa totonatappiye.
muu tar makattipaliye.   95

machi esakunappi kwekitup otimakkenatappiye.
"kilu tar pulekanpa nekati ipkuto taylemosunye."
machi esakunappiye kwekitup otimaysi.
kilu nele niakkwa nele ulu yakineye.

kilu tar pulekana tar kalu ainisa takkekwaye.   100
kilu kalu pilli saitilekemaiye.
pela wiasalikwale tar kalu pilli saitimai machi neka pali taynatappiye.

kilu niakwa nele tar kalu pilli ainisaye.
makattipaliye kilu tar pulekana sunnamakkekwichiye.
"machi esakunappiye?"   105

man esa ulu tarpa kinnemaiye.
man esa ulu tarpa totonatappiye.
muu tar makattipaliye.

kilu tar pulekanaye, olo panter kalukana ainisa takkeye.
machi kwekitup otimaysiye.   110

Machi Esakunappiye is watching this as he goes along.   80
Sacred Uncle Shark's silver boat is coming into sight, Sacred Uncle
   Devilfish's silver boat is coming into sight.

Sacred Uncle Devil's boats zigzag past each other.
The boats dance along on the waves.
They circle along on the waves.
Machi watches this as he goes along.   85

Machi Esakunappi sees this as he goes along.
Many boats are coming into sight.
Uncle's Sea People's boats are coming into sight.

On the waves the boats dance along.
On the waves the boats rise along.   90
The waves are standing up.
Machi watches this as he goes along.

The waves are fluttering by.
On the waves the boat dances along in the breeze.
Out on the waves.   95

Machi Esakunappi gathers heart as he goes along.
"I will dwell with those valiant uncles it seems also."
Machi Esakunappiye is sitting gathering heart.
Within Sacred Uncle Devil the Sacred One's boat.

The stronghold of the valiant Uncles came into sight it seems.   100
The towers of Uncle's stronghold are fogged in.
The towers of the stronghold are all covered with drizzle they are fogged
   in Machi sees this as he goes along.

The towers of Sacred Uncle Devil's stronghold came into sight.
Out on the sea the valiant Uncles are standing speaking.
"Machi Esakunappiye (they call to him)?"   105

The silver boat is speeding along in the breeze.
The silver boat dances along in the breeze.
Out on the waves.

The golden flags, of the valiant Uncles' strongholds came into sight it
   seems.
Machi is sitting gathering heart.   110

kilu niakkwa nele kalu poosumpakanti olo kannelakanti neka.
oipote tayleye.
machi kwekitup otimaysiye.

kilu pulekana nekase walamaysaye kilu tar kalu pilli saitilekemai pela
    wiasalikwaleye.
Machi esakunappiye neka tar pali taynatappiye.

kilu niakkwa nele walepunkana pattemekwisaye.   115
man esa ulu naikutappiye.
e esana tupakanti iimayteye.
ulu urmola tupakanti uurmakkenakusaye.
man esa ulu tar nakutappiye.
kilu tar kalu pillisekakwaye.   120
machi neka tar pali taynatappiye.

kilu niakkwa nele walepunkana pattemaiye.
"tule pinikana nonikki takkeye.
kilu niakkwa nele machi pinikan tar otenonikki takke."
walepunkan tar oimayteye.   125

pela nitarpaki nele tar walepunkana pattemaiye.
kilu nalikka nele walepunkan pattemaiye.
machi esakunappiye takkemalattiye, muu tar makattipaliye.

kilu nele niakkwa nele sunnamakkakekwichikwaye.
kilu nitarpaki nele   na machi esakunappiye ekichekwichiye, kilu
    seka.   130
"na pe ipe apeke."

machi olo pakkiye machi mani esakunappi wisokekwichi kilu.
kilu niakkwa neletinaye.
"walepunkana na peka ukkoeye."

"we walepunkana kwen apesuliye."   135
machi esakunappiye sunnamakkekwichiye.
"omekana nuekana kwen takkesulikwaye.

ome wekimalatti tar nikkueka tanikkisuliye," machi esakunappiye,
    kiluka sunnamakkekwichiye.

kilute walepunkan oilemakkali olo kansupillipaliye.
walepunkan ampakuemaiye.   140

Sacred Uncle Devil's stronghold his abodes are all lit up with golden
candles.
It seems like it is dawn.
Machi is sitting gathering heart.

They arrived at the home of the valiant Uncles the towers of Uncles'
stronghold are fogged in and all covered with drizzle.
Machi Esakunappiye watches this as he goes along.

Sacred Uncle Devil's spouses were descending.   115
The silver boat arrived there at the dock.
The ropes of its mooring sound out.
The ropes of its sails were making noise.
The silver boat arrived there at the dock.
It arrived at the towers of Uncle's stronghold it did.   120
Machi watches this as he goes along.

Sacred Uncle Devil's spouses are descending.
"New people have come it seems.
Sacred Uncle Devil came and lowered (brought) a new machi it seems."
The spouses sound out.   125

All Sacred Devilfish's spouses are descending.
All Sacred Uncle Shark's spouses are descending.
In order to see Machi Esakunappiye, out on the waves.

Sacred Uncle Devil the Sacred One stands up to speak.
Sacred Uncle Devilfish   is now standing asking Uncle, about Machi
Esakunappi.   130
"I want yours (Machi to marry my daughter)."

Uncle is standing informing Golden Machi Silver Machi Esakunappi.
Sacred Uncle Devil.
"I will give you spouses."

"I do not want these spouses."   135
Machi Esakunappiye is standing speaking.
"I do not like these pretty women.

I have not come in order to marry women from here," Machi
Esakunappiye, is standing speaking to Uncle.

And Uncle is lining up the spouses on a golden bench.
The spouses are in place.   140

"na pe takketikwapa na walepunkana na pe suo takkeye."
machi esakunappi aka kilu nele niakkwa nele sunnamakkekwichiye.

machi esakunappiye sunnamakkekwichiye.
"kilu nele niakkwa nele pe siskwa an apesulimokarkeye, ansikki na kwen
    takkesulikeye.

pela asu matare an takkeye.   145
an omeka kwen saer taylesurye."
machi esakunappiye, kiluka sunnamakkekwichiye.

"ome walakwen tanikki tayleye soke.
we   pe nappa nekakineye.
we omekwa weki neka ipkumaiye," kilu sunnamakkeye.   150

"muu kunwa nana neka ipkumai, a nekaki walepunkana tar mai tanikki
    takkenaye."
machi esakunappiye pali takkesiye.
ome sermesetanikkwaye.
pela mani takutikki olua tummakana oipyetanikki takkekwichiye.

"tulerpa tayleye," pinsakwichi machi esakunappiye.   155
"weti ome ipkupi tayleye."
kwekitup otimaysiye.

kilu niakkwa neleka soke tayleye, "we omekwa weti kaoye."

kilu niakkwa neleye.
"tuuki ittomaloeye toati na peka ukkoeye."   160
kilu niakkwa nele, machi esakunappi aka sunnamakkekwichikwaye,
    muu tar makattipaliye.

na walepunkanatika innakwa ittoalimalaye.
kilu pulekanaye.
inna ittoepukkwakusaye.

kilu tar pulekana, kilu nalikka nelekante pali taypukkwaye kilu
    nitarpaki nelekana pali taypukkwaye.   165

"Take spouses to your liking see."
Sacred Uncle Devil the Sacred One is standing speaking to Machi
   Esakunappi.

Machi Esakunappiye is standing speaking.
"Sacred Uncle Devil the Sacred One I do not want your daughter, she
   does not please me.

I see that they all have flat noses.   145
I do not care to take these women."
Machi Esakunappiye, is standing speaking to Uncle.

"One woman is coming it seems say.
She   is of your land.
This woman is dwelling here," Uncle says.   150

"She is dwelling with the Mother of the Sparklings of the Waves, the
   spouses are coming from that house it seems."
Machi Esakunappiye is sitting watching.
The woman comes drifting along.
All her pale silver her big gold (jewelry) can be seen coming reflecting
   along.

"This one is indeed a tule (Kuna person) it seems," Machi Esakunappi
   is standing thinking.   155
"I want to possess (marry) this woman see "
He is sitting gathering heart.

He says to Sacred Uncle Devil it seems, "I want to grab (marry) this
   woman."

Sacred Uncle Devil (says).
"Let us taste our libation (to determine) who will be given now to
   you (who will win the woman)."   160
Sacred Uncle Devil, is standing speaking to Machi Esakunappi, out
   on the waves.

Now the spouses together are tasting (drinking) chicha.
There are many valiant Uncles.
They all tasted chicha.

There are many valiant Uncles, there are sacred Uncle Sharks who
   watch there are Sacred Uncle Devilfish who watch.   165

kurkur nokaki ittokoeye, "toakine opinemalotipaye?"
kilu tar pulekan sunnamakkepukkwaye.

kurkur noka ittoesokkaliye.

puna olo makkili sopikwaye.
"melle kallakkuena yerpan tayleye."   170
kilu tar oimakkepukkwaye.
kilu tar pulekantinaye.

"machi esakunappiye kurkur noka kasana yerpana ati ipkuosuliye."
kilumala per oimayteye, muu tar makattipali, "machi esakunappiye, ome
    nikkuesokkaliye."

muu kunwa nana pali takkesikwaye.   175
na walepunkan pali takkesiye.
muu kati, walepunkwa yaakwa tar ukkesokkaliye.

"toa pe ittoemekwisamalaye?
toapa pete kuekwichiye?"
kilu tar pulekan otimayteye.   180
kilu pulekan oimakkepukkwaye.

machi esakunappiye tuu   poomettese pupawar aipilisaye tuu tarpo
    ittoesokkali.
olo makkili sopise kurkur.
kurkur noka ukkenonikkikwaye.

olo makkili sopi e pokwa na penekuali machi esakunappiye kurkur
    nokapa penekukwichiye.   185

machi esakunappi yeti.
pela kurkur noka otinnokwichikwaye puna olo makkili sopi.
kurkur noka katappiye.

machi esakunappiye walepunkan annikka susa.
kurkur noka pela otinnotekusaye.   190
kilu tar pulekan oimayteye.

olo makkili sopi na ipkunonikki.
machi esakunappiye tar muu makattipaliye.

They will taste in the *kurkur* cup (type of ritual drinking cup), "Who will
 win?"
All the valiant Uncles speak.

They are about to taste the *kurkur* cup.

Sister Golden Makkili Sopikwaye (the wife of Machi Esakunappi drinks).
"Do not lose."   170
The Uncles all sound out (they imagine Machi Esakunappi thinks this).
The many valiant Uncles.

"If Machi Esakunappiye does not finish the *kurkur* cup he will not
 possess her."
The Uncles sound out, out on the waves, "Machi Esakunappi, is about to
 marry the woman."

The Mother of the Sparklings of the Waves is sitting watching.   175
The spouses are sitting watching.
The one belonging to the sea (the sea turtle), the spouse is about to give
 up her daughter.

"Who was tasting with you?
Who will beat you"
The valiant Uncles sound out.   180
The many valiant Uncles all sound out.

Machi Esakunappiye twirled toward   the libation vessel the two of
 them (he and his wife) are about to taste the libation together.
Golden Makkili Sopi (is given) the *kurkur* cup.
They came and gave him the *kurkur* cup.

Golden Makkili Sopi the two of them are competing Machi Esakunappi
 is standing competing with the *kurkur* cup.   185

Machi Esakunappi that one.
Is standing drying up (finishing off) the *kurkur* cup while Sister Golden
 Makkili Sopi.
Still has some there in the *kurkur* cup.

Machi Esakunappi took his spouse's (cup away).
He dried the *kurkur* cup all up.   190
The valiant Uncles sound out.

He came and possessed Golden Makkili Sopi.
Machi Esakunappi out on the waves.

PART III

Women's Songs

Figure 18. Women ritually drinking chicha during puberty festivities

Chapter 11

Chicha Song

Performed by Justina Pineda Castrellan

During puberty festivities, in addition to the ritual cutting of a young girl's hair and the performance of long chants by the master of ceremonies, the *kantule*, there are various other activities that occur. One of these is the performance of chants and songs, by both men and women, for the pleasure and amusement of a gathered audience, as well as representatives of the spirit world who listen in.[1] Spirits are believed to drink chicha, get drunk, and enjoy verbal art and verbal play and humor, just as humans do.

The short song presented here was performed by Justina Pineda Castrellan, in 1970, in my house in Mulatuppu. Justina was in her teens at the time and passing through Mulatuppu, where I was carrying out research. She was from the village of Caiman Nuevo, near the Gulf of Uraba in Colombia. While most Kuna live in Panama, there are also Kuna villages in Colombia, and the Kuna believe that they migrated to their present location from Colombia.

Puberty rites and festivities are perhaps the most important of all Kuna rituals, and several other texts presented in this book describe them in various ways. This is the only occasion when the Kuna are supposed to drink alcoholic beverages in great quantities. The consumption of alcohol, especially native made chicha, is a very important part of the ritual.[2] The song presented here is a metacommunicative description of one aspect of these rites and festivities, competitive drinking, from the perspective of a female participant, a young woman, whose ritual name, used in the text, is Golden Nitinkitili. It describes how the women, elegantly dressed in their finest clothing, sit next to one another on benches and get drunk. The goal is to finish up one's cup first, before the others. Meanwhile other women, as well as men, all very drunk, perform various kinds of ceremonial dances as traditional Kuna flutes are played.

There is a bustling of activity, including ritual eating, drinking, talking, laughing, joking, singing, dancing, and playful and not so playful arguing. Women sit among family and friends whose company they enjoy. And they display a verbal abililty and exuberance comparable to that of Kuna men.

GRAMMAR, STYLE, AND VOCABULARY

Since this chicha song is addressed to the spirit world, it shares certain stylistic features with the curing and magical chants presented in this book. It is told in the third person, even though it is about the chanter. Morpheme and word final vowels, typically deleted in everyday speech, are often retained. The word *kue* "do," often follows verbs and this elongates poetic lines. Thus, line 31:

She sat down there she did.

And line 50:

Now the woman feels happy, she feels happy doing various
  things now she did she does.

The singer/song quotes herself and others, as in lines 47 and 48:

"The woman is now whirling herself around she is she is."
The woman says she does.

This song performance uses the sound *j* (as in the English word "join"), otherwise never found in the Kuna language.

Most Kuna would not understand this song. This is due mainly to its metaphorical and esoteric vocabulary. Metaphors include *tinamakke* "dry" for "drink;" *aiteke* "land" for "sit down;" and *kalu* "stronghold" for "house." Words that are esoteric, in that they are found only in chants addressed to the spirit world, include *panja*, which I translate as "until"; *tuu*, which I translate as "libation"; and *yapakilakwa*, which I translate as "little one." *Piryamakke* "whirl" and *siamakke* "bounce" describe ceremonial dances performed at puberty rites festivities. Objects, such as cups, are described as being "live," because they, like humans, have spirits or souls, and indeed are the spirits being addressed in this song.

Olokwagdi de Akwanusadup's illustration of this song shows women, in their finest attire, including large gold earrings, noserings, gold breast plates, bead necklaces, wrist and ankle bracelets, head kerchiefs, skirts, and of course, beautiful molas (fig. 18). They are drinking chicha competitively, sitting and standing next to large jars that contain chicha. They are clearly enjoying themselves. My photographs show women dressed for puberty festivities and participating in them (photos 24–27).

Here is the chicha song, as it was performed by Justina Pineda Castrellan.

Kuna

tuu napsali pomettekana, an aitoe te maite.
punatolati nuale sikwite kue.

ipa panja panja meleke, e kwenatti pomette onote.
"tinamakke" punatola soke kue.

na punatola nuale sikwite kue. 5

innakana pillimaite kue.
punatola aipanesikwite kue.
punatolati nue nate.

ipe sintisi sola meleke.
puna mattuti tappi kue. 10
puna mattuti sikwite.
kalu ipkana kalu pillikana nueti.

na ipe panja panja meleke.
punatola nuelokoe soketipa.
patto tio neleti ani punatola arpa ani kute kua. 15
na takke punatolati kue kuye.
puna ipa panja panja pilliki.
"puna nuale nonikki."
punatola soke.

puna nuale noniku, noka tulemala palitakkesikwite kue. 20
inna tuu napsali pomettekana, an itu iti maite ku.
na palita sikwite.
ipe napsali nokakampa, punatola penekusoke kua.
punatola nuale sii.

punatola tina weki. 25
punatola kue suli sokele kuye.
"ammolokankala napsali pomettekanti unni tinamakkarsuli."
punatolati soke sokkua.
punatolati tinamakkali kuye.

punatolati tuu napsali pomettekana yalapa. 30
punatola aititappi kua.
punatola mattuletappi kuye.

English

The libation's earthen vessels, I lift them up.
And the pretty woman (I) sits down (in the chicha house) she does.

Until what day will it (the festival) last, the family's vessels come out.
"For drying (drinking)" the woman says she does.

Now the pretty woman sits down she does.   5

The chicha is all lined up it is.
The woman is sitting swaying she is.
And the pretty woman goes (to the chicha house).

She sits herself down.
And the short woman is there she is.   10
And the short woman sits down.
Inside the stronghold next to the pretty walls of the stronghold.

Now until what day will it (the festival) last.
Whatever will the pretty woman say.
And for God I the woman am working I am I am.   15
Now the woman sees this she does she does.
The woman until what day.
"The pretty woman came."
The woman says.

When the pretty women comes, she sits watching over the live cups
    she does.   20
The chicha's the libation's earthen vessels, are in line in front of me
    they are.
Now she sits watching over them.
With the earthen cups, the woman competes (at drinking) she does.
The pretty woman is seated there.

And the woman is here.   25
If the woman is not present it is said it is.
"If the aunts (family) do not come to dry up the earthen vessels."
The woman says she does.
And the woman is drying them up she is.

And the woman is (all drunk) with the libation beside the earthen
    vessels.   30
The woman landed (sat down) there she did.
The woman lowered herself down there she did.

ipe napsali pomettekan, unni tinamakkoeye.
unni unni sokali nokakan tinamakkekwichikusa.
inna napsali pomette yalapar kusa.   35

na tuu napsali pomette sokele tii.
pela tinamaysa kue.

na ipa toletolepa wala.
ipe pua tola tina kuye.
ipe pua sailakine ipe tole sailapa walapali kuye.   40
ipe toletolepa wala aknue makkalikua tule kue.
uka tulemala pupa piryamakkali sokali kuye.
punatola puna mattulekwichikusa.
uka tulemar yalapaliye.

puna mattuletappiku.   45
uka tulemar yalapar.
"pupa piryamakkali na kute kue."
punatola soke kua.
na pupa piryamakkar na kusa kuye.
na puna werikunai, ipekan welikwar sailakwa imakke na kusa kua.   50
uka tulemar yalapa, punatola kueye.

na ipe tolepa walapa imakkali kua.
ipe toletole walapa pupa siamakkenai.
punatola kue.

ipe toletolepa walapali pupa siamakkali kua.   55
ampa olo kana palitakkali kua.

ipe toletolepa walapa.

walakan wilikana.
ani olo turpakan imakkaliye.

ani olo turpakana imakke na kusa.   60
punatola nuale tappi ku.
olo kaseli nokakan tinamakkekwamala.
uka tulemar welimakkekwichi ku.

The sacred earthen vessels, will be all dried up.
And they were standing drying up all the cups.
Beside the chicha's earthen vessels they were.   35

Now the libation's earthen vessels it is said.
She dried them all off she did.

Now there are various *tole* flutes (being played).
She is next to the sacred live house pole she is.
She is next to the sacred principal house pole next to the sacred principal
     tole flute she is.   40
The various sacred *tole* flutes are playing they are.
The relatives (boys) are whirling themselves around (dancing
     ceremonially) it is said it is.
The woman was standing lowering herself down she was.
Beside the relatives.

The woman lowered herself down there she did.   45
Beside the relatives.
"The woman is now whirling herself around she is she is."
The woman says she does.
Now she is whirling herself around now she was she is.
Now the woman feels happy, she feels happy doing various things now
     she did she does.   50
Beside the relatives, the woman is.

Now the various sacred *tole* flutes are sounding out they are.
Beside the various sacred *tole* flutes she is bouncing herself (type of
     ceremonial dancing).
The woman is.

Beside the various flutes she is bouncing herself she is.   55
And she is watching over the golden benches she is.

Beside the various sacred *tole* flutes.

My *winkwa* necklace's.
Golden fruit (beads) are sounding out.

My various golden fruits (beads) are sounding out they are.   60
The pretty girl is there she is.
We will dry up the golden *kaseli* cups we will.
The relatives are standing feeling happy they are.

ipe tinaki, olo sikkiliti nokakan tinamakkekwichi kua.
ilapa, ukakanapa naaletikine.   65
aa tinamaysa kua.
puna nuale tappimariye.

puna nuale sikwite kua.

olo sikkili nokakana apitakkesikwitepali.
yapakilakan iesa.   70
"punatola yapakilakana kwena wisikusasuliku."
punatola soke kue.

na punatola sokekua, "na olo paseli nokakan tinamakkesikkwitepali."

olo nitinkitili kwayee.
"anise irmakkesikwiteye."   75

punatola nuale siiti.
"uka tulemarpakkar penekuesikwisa."
punatola kue sokkua.
yer ittosmala, welikwar ittosikwite.

The are standing, drying up the sacred *tinaki* cups the golden *sikki* cups
    they are.
Each of the relatives, one by one after her.   65
They finished drying they did.
The pretty woman is there she is.

The pretty woman sits down she does.

She is sitting waiting again for the golden *sikki* cups.
She forgot her little ones (children).   70
"The woman completely lost consciousness of her little ones (she is
    completely drunk)."
The woman says she does.

Now the woman says she does, "Now I am sitting drying up the golden
    paseli cups again."

Golden Nitinkitili (woman's name) she is.
"The golden jars are sitting lined up to me."   75

The pretty woman is sitting there.
"Together with all the relatives sitting competing (to see who can drink
    more chicha)."
The woman does she says she does.
They felt happy, they are sitting feeling happy.

Figure 19. Young girl hanging clothes on a line

Chapter 12

Three Kuna Lullabies

Performed by
Julieta Quijano, Brieta Quijano, and Donalda Garcia

The best known form of Kuna visual art is the mola, an appliqué and reverse appliqué blouse made, worn, and sold by Kuna women. Kuna women are also verbal artists and perform a variety of Kuna genres, including myths, counsels, curing and magical chants, chicha songs,[1] and lullabies.

Lullabies are omnipresent in Kuna villages. If you walk through a Kuna village, especially in the morning when men are at work, you hear singing coming from almost every house. These are the voices of women, from young girls to quite old grandmothers, singing to little babies, their children, brothers, sisters, or grandchildren, to keep them calm and put them to sleep. Lullabies are often called *koe pippi* "little baby," named for the addressee, who is explicitly referred to in the song. In the performance of lullabies, the singer holds the baby in her lap in a hammock or sits next to it, moving the hammock back and forth and shaking a rattle.

Lullabies have certain basic themes. The baby is counseled not to be sad and not to cry, that it will soon grow up and perform adult tasks, and that its father is off working in the jungle or fishing. This is the first of many counsels that children hear in their lives. Verbal counsels constitute a very important Kuna verbal practice and are performed to humans of all ages and roles and to spirits as well. In lullabies, as in all counsels, there is improvisation to fit the actual situation—whether the singer is a mother, sister, or aunt; whether the baby is a boy or a girl; whether those off at work are fathers, uncles, or brothers; whether they are farming in the jungle, fishing, or working in Panama City. The description is reflexive in that the singer describes what she is doing at the moment of the performance, as well as what the relevant others are doing.

The language of lullabies is that of colloquial Kuna, intelligible to all Kuna, with certain stylistic features shared with other forms of Kuna singing and chanting. Morpheme and especially word final vowels are typically not deleted so that they occur in full form, for example *nana* "mother" rather than *nan*. The suffix -*ye*, which has an optative, subjunctive, as well as quotative function, is used with frequency, especially at the ends of lines. Verse or stanzalike units are terminated with a long lulling and soothing *mmmm* or *eeee*. As in most Kuna chanting, speaking, and singing, voices are quoted directly rather than referred to indirectly.

Lullabies describe the idealized role of men and women in Kuna society. Women wash clothes for men and serve them beverages. They make molas in their leisure time. Men hunt and fish and farm in the jungle, and go to Panama City for long periods of time, leaving their wives and children alone.

Olokwagdi de Akwanusadup's illustrations depict the themes of the lullabies, a young girl hanging clothes she has just washed (fig. 19), a young boy fishing off a dock (fig. 20), and a young girl making a mola (fig. 1, p. xii). In the sky above the girl, a smiling human face, the sun personified, is looking happily down at this Kuna scene. Children are expected to perform adult activities from a young age, and these lullabies and illustrations of them depict this expectation. The lullabies and the illustrations also portray a simple, innocent, balanced, harmonious, almost naive view of childhood. My photograph shows a woman, Benilda Quijano, with her baby (photo 28).

The first two lullabies were performed in 1970, by two sisters, Julieta and Brieta Quijano, in Mulatuppu; the third, in 1979, was performed by Donalda García, also in Mulatuppu.[2]

Figure 20. *Young boy fishing off a Kuna dock*

Lullaby, performed by Julieta Quijano

Kuna

koe pipiye.
ani okormainaye.
yo tunkupi sokele.
kilomarka mol enukkoye.
kilolomala okopkwici kuoe.   5
mmmm
kilolomar tiwalapa nanamokoe.
susumarka mol enukkoe.
tiwalapa yokkukwici kuoe.
mmmm
melle poeye.
ani wiale pe takkenaye.   10
peka namakkenaiye.
opoekwiciye.
kwenattikanase kolemokoeye.
"nana nateye.
nana sappurupa nateye.   15
nana na solapa wialeke pe takkenaye.
pe opokepiesuliye."
mmmm

English

Little baby.
Is lying bawling.
When you are grown up say.
You will wash clothes for your uncles.
And you will stand serving beverages to your uncles you will.   5
mmmm
While your uncles go to the river also.
You will wash clothes for your brothers.
You will stray at the river you will.
mmmm
Do not cry.
I am caring for you you see.   10
I am singing for you.
As you cry.
You will also tell your brothers.
"Mother went away.
Mother went to the jungle.   15
In Mother's absence I am caring for you.
And I don't want you to cry."
mmmm

Lullaby, performed by Brieta Quijano

Kuna

koe pipiye koe pipiye.
papa sappurupa nateye.
papati pemalaka kottenateye.
"masi sikkenakoloeye."
papa pemalaka kottenateye.   5
nika pipiye.
eeee
nana pemar wile takketii nanatii.
pemar sattoetina natee koe pipiye.
eeee
yo yaypalesatipeleye.
nanakala ua soenaoeye.   10
ani papa pepoki papauna kwiskuetimarmoka koe pipiye.
eeee
nanakala pe mola enukkenamaloye.
nana pemar wiletii.
nana pemarse kortikutoe koe pipiye.
   eeee
eka popisuli nana apetii kutoe.   15
nika pipi tata nateye.
tata Julioti sapurupa nateye.
eeee
koe pipiye.
mmmm
papa kottenateye.
"mimmimalakala ua soenakolo" papa kottenateye.   20
koe pipiye.
eeee
mu pekatii.
tiwalapa mu peka umolakala yokkue mu pemalaka nateye.
koe pipiye.
melle poeye.   25
mmmm
koe nika pipiye.
nika macitola pipi pemar wile taytikutoeye.

English

Little baby little baby.
Father went to the jungle.
And Father told you as he left.
"I am going to cut plantains."
Father told you as he left.   5
Little nephew.
eeee
Mother feels sorry for you Mother does.
She is doing things for you little baby.
eeee
When you are bigger.
You will go fishing for Mother.   10
Together with Father you will be and you will help Father little baby.
eeee
Mother will wash clothes for you.
Mother is caring for you.
Mother is calling to you little baby.
eeee
Mother does not want you to cry.   15
Little nephew Grandfather went away.
And Grandfather Julio went to the jungle.
eeee
Little baby.
mmmm
Father shouted as he left.
"I am going fishing for my children" Father shouted as he left.   20
Little baby.
eeee
And your grandmother.
Your grandmother strayed at the river (in order to get) the clothes your
    grandmother went for you.
Little baby.
Do not cry.   25
mmmm
Little baby nephew.
Nephew little boy I am feeling sorry for you.

iamala unnikusale kusapinnemokoye.
nanakala ua soenaoeye.
koe pipiye.   30
eeee
tata nonikki sokele tata pepo naoe.
tata sappurupa pepo naoe koe pipiye.
ammolo pipi peka ukachiki nakualiye.

When you are as big as your brothers.
You will go fishing for your mother.
Little baby.   30
eeee
When Grandfather returns say you and Grandfather will go together.
You and Grandfather will go together to the jungle little baby.
Your little aunt is with you in the hammock.

Lullaby, performed by Donalda Garcia

Kuna

koe pippiye.
nana peka nakusaye.
koe pippi wialeke poenai takkeye.
mmmm
punolo pipiye.
naka pippi nikkusaye.   5
apparmakkekwakwicimokaye.
ammolokana wialeke pe takketiye.
an koe punolo pipi naka pipi nikkusaye.
mmmm
kwenattikana unnikusamokaye.
totoetki pinsaekusamokaye.   10
koe pipiye.
papa yokkusaye.
papa sapurupali neka iskanpa yokkutiye.
anti sorpa peka pal epinsanaiye.
papa kwena takke suli ante takkenaiye.   15
sappurupaliye.
"okopa ollomakkenaekoloeye."
papakwa ipi piekwakwicikwanateye.
mmmm
macitola pipi kue sokenaye.
papapa yokkuti pe kumokoenaye.   20
sappurupali neka iskanpa yalumakketi pe kumokoenaye.
emitina teki suliye.
mimmi punoloye.
peti nek uyaki sikoeye.
mola pipi makkesiiye.   25
nana yalapali siymokoeye.
ammolokana pese kolemokoeye.
mmmm
punolo pipi koe pipi mekenonikkiye.
naka pipi nikkuenonikkiye.
kwenattikana yalapa walakwena ei yaypalekekwatanikki pe takkeye.   30
koe punolo pipiye.
mmmm
mola pipi enukkoeye.
tii walapa yokkueti kuoeye.
kwenattikanapaliye.
mola pipi enukketi kumokoeye.   35
nana walakwena pe otummoekwatanikkiye.

English

Little baby.
Mother is with you in your hammock.
Little baby she is sorry to see you cry.
mmmm
Little girl.
You already have little feet.   5
You are able to stand running also.
Your aunts are sorry to see you (cry).
My little baby girl already has little feet.
mmmm
You are also as big as your relatives.
You are able to play also.   10
Little baby.
Father strayed.
Father strayed far away in the jungle.
I am thinking of him for you.
I see that Father is not here.   15
(He went) To the jungle.
"I will go and clear out the coconut farms."
Father uttered as he left.
mmmm
If you were a little boy say.
You would also stray with Father you would.   20
You would also wander far away in the jungle.
Now it is not that way.
(You are) a girl child.
And you must remain in the house.
You are sitting making a little mola.   25
You must sit beside Mother as well.
Your aunts will call on you also.
mmmm
Little girl little newly born baby.
Your little legs are coming along.
I see you growing beside your relatives.   30
Little baby girl.
mmmm
You will wash your little mola.
You will stray to the river you will.
With your relatives.
In order to wash your little mola you will.   35
Mother is raising you alone.

ei punolo pipi yaypakusa nana takketimokaye.
mmmm
kilolomala okopoeye.
kilolomala tanikki sokeleye.
kilolomala okopekwakwici kuoeye.   40
masiki okunnoeye.
kilolomala tanikki sokeleye.
mmmm
kwenattikana pese koloeye.
"anka kopeti weekweleye."
kwenattikana pese koloeye.   45
kwenattikana masiki okunnoye.
mmmm
mimmi punolo pipiye.
ani punolo pipi mekenonikkiye.
koe pipi punoloye.
mmmm

And Mother already sees you a grown little girl.
mmmm
You must serve beverages to your uncles.
When your uncles return (from work in the jungle) say.
You must stand serving beverages to your uncles you must.   40
You must serve them food.
When your uncles return say.
 mmmm
Your relatives will call you.
"Bring me a beverage."
Your relatives will call you.   45
You must serve food to the relatives.
mmmm
Child little girl.
My little girl lying here.
Little baby girl.
mmmm

Figure 21. Parakeet on dock overlooks the sea

Chapter 13

Counsel to a Parakeet

Performed by Justina Pineda Castrellan

This short song, a humorous and pleasant sounding counsel to a parakeet, is akin to lullabies.[1] It was performed in 1970 by Justina Pineda Castrellan, the same person who performed the chicha song.[2]

The Kuna keep parakeets as pets. They catch them in the jungle and keep them in their houses. They are very fond of them. This fondness is expressed in this song. Like lullabies to children, this song counsels the parakeet not to be sad and not to cry and promises it that it will get food, when it gets a Panamanian owner. The Kuna often sell their parakeets to Panamanians, who also keep them as pets. The close relationship that the Kuna feel exists between humans and animals is depicted in this song, which counsels a parakeet, in the Kuna language, just as it might a human being.

Like lullabies, the language of this song is everyday colloquial Kuna and is understandable to all Kuna. The word used for Panamanian in this song is *waka*, which means foreigner. Panamanians are the Kuna's most significant foreigners.

Olokwagdi de Akwanusadup's illustration of this song (fig. 21) is a harmonious picture of a parakeet next to his (and Kuna) food, a banana, and a portion of a Kuna traditional house, overlooking the sea complete with a sandy beach, seagulls flying overhead, a large boat, perhaps Kuna owned perhaps belonging to Colombian sailors, passing through to buy coconuts, a familiar sight in Kuna Yala, and a Kuna canoe, all bathed in the light of a rising (or setting) sun.

Here is the song.

Kuna

kwili patto kwarukwa.
waka ulu takkoeye.
prrrr

kwili tuttu.
waka ulupa naoe.   5
nanapati sokele.
ukkur mesosulina.
prrrr

emiski pani ukkur mesesisunna.
nanapa poetii.
prrrr

waka neypa nat soker.   10
matu kunnena.
matu kunnesioe.
matuka poesioeye.
prrrr

emiski wiles ittoke.
mas koro kunnetpa.   15
poesii.
prrrr.

English

Parakeet is still newly born.
It will see the Panamanian boat.
prrrr

Parakeet is tender.
It will go to the Panamanian boat.   5
If it gets to its mother.
It will not be hungry.
prrrr

Now you are truly hungry.
And crying for your mother.
prrrr

When you get to the Panamanians say.   10
You will eat bread.
You will sit eating bread.
And you will sit crying with the bread.
prrrr

Now you are sorrowful.
In order to eat ripe bananas.   15
You are sitting crying.
prrrr.

Notes

Chapter 1. Introduction

1. In addition to viewing the texts in this book, they can be listened to on the Archive of the Indigenous Languages of Latin America (AILLA) , on the World Wide Web, at www.ailla.org.

2. I am grateful to Adolfo Constenla Umaña for discussions about this question.

3. In my translations, as well as transcriptions, I have benefited greatly from the collaboration with two Kuna friends and consultants, Hortencio Martínez and the late Anselmo Urrutia, as well as much fruitful correspondence and collaboration with Mac Chapin and James Howe.

4. See Parker and Neal (1977) and Salvador (1978, 1997).

5. For another transcription system, see the articles in Salvador (1997).

6. Research for this book was supported by the National Endowment for the Humanities, a National Institute of Mental Health small grant, the National Science Foundation, the John Simon Guggenheim Memorial Foundation, and the University of Texas. For other relevant publications dealing with Kuna oral literature, see Kramer (1970); Kungiler (1997); Howe (1986); Howe, Sherzer, and Chapin (1980); McCosker (1974); Salvador (1997); and Sherzer (1983, 1990). The book has benefited from comments by Jill Brody, Mac Chapin, James Howe, Mari Lyn Salvador, and Dina Sherzer. I am most grateful for the magnificent editorial and production assistance of Virginia Hagerty and Heather Teague of the Teresa Lozano Long Institute of Latin American Studies, and Teresa Wingfield of the University of Texas Press.

Chapter 2. *The One-Eyed Grandmother*, told by Pedro Arias

1. Thompson (1961), tale types 300 and 327/327A. See also Tatar (1987). Adolfo Costenla Umaña recorded a quite similar story in 1976 from a Spanish-speaking, non-indigenous Costa Rican, Mayro Loaiza. Taggart (1986) recorded a version of it in Spain and Mexico in Spanish, and in Mexico in Nahuatl-speaking communities. He points out how it is adapted to Nahuat social structure and cultural practices, including gender relations. This story is also widespread in Mayan-speaking communities (personal communication from Nicholas Hopkins; see also Peñalosa 1996). Laura Martin (1997) recorded it among the Mayan-speaking Mocho.

2. Compare with the grandmother of the "Hot Pepper Story" in Sherzer (1990), chap. 6.

3. In chaps. 6 and 10, I translate *nia* as "devil."

4. Wafer (1970 [1699]) provides a seventeenth-century description.

Chapter 4. *The Turtle Story*, told by Chief Nipakkinya

1. Thompson (1961), tale type 1074.

2. This is perhaps a Kuna version of the widespread eating-contest story. See Thompson (1961), tale type 1088.

3. See Sherzer (1995).

4. This is Chief Nipakkinya's structuring of this story. Other Kuna versions keep them separate. See Wassen (1937), who recorded the second episode as a complete story on the island of Ustuppu.

5. An earlier and different version of this chapter appeared as Sherzer (1997).

Chapter 5. *The Way of the Turtle*, told by Pedro Arias

1. Chap. 2.

2. This is the land turtle or tortoise, which the Kuna call *yarmoro*, and not the sea turtle, which the Kuna call *yaukka* and which is the central figure in the story in chap. 10. Both of these animals are important to the Kuna and figure in their literature.

3. See Sherzer (1990), chaps. 4 and 7.

4. Thompson (1961), tale type 60.

5. Sherzer (1995).

Chapter 6. *Counsel to the Way of the Devil Medicine*, performed by Anselmo Urrutia

1. Chap. 8.

2. Urrutia and Sherzer (2000).

3. See Holmer (1958) and Severi and Gomez (1983).

Chapter 7. *The Way of Cooling Off*, performed by Pranki Pilos

1. Sherzer (1990), chap. 8.

2. The word *waiye* is often intoned at the beginning of magical and curing chants.

Chapter 8. *The Way of the Rattlesnake*, performed by Olowiktinappi

1. Sherzer (1990), chap. 5.

Chapter 10. *The Way of the Sea Turtle*, performed by Tiowilikinya

1. See Sherzer (1983), chap. 5 and chaps. 9 and 11 of this book.

2. Arias and Chapin (1972); Kungiler (1997).

3. Carr (1967).

Chapter 11. *Chicha Song*, performed by Justina Pineda Castrellan

1. See chap. 10.
2. See chap. 9.

Chapter 12. *Three Kuna Lullabies*, performed by Julieta Quijano, Brieta Quijano, and Donalda Garcia

1. See chap. 11.
2. For more Kuna lullabies and a discussion of them, see McCosker (1974).

Chapter 13. *Counsel to a Parakeet*, performed by Justina Pineda Castrellan

1. See chap. 12.
2. See chap. 11.

References

Arias, Albertino, and Mac Chapin
  1972 *Yaukki namakket (El canto de la tortuga)*. Unpublished ms.
Carr, Archie
  1967 *The Sea Turtle: So Excellent a Fishe*. Austin: University of Texas Press.
Holmer, Nils M.
  1958 *Nia-ikala: Canto mágico para curar la locura*. Etnologiska Studier 23. Göteburg: Göteburgs Etnografiska Museum.
Howe, James
  1986 *The Kuna Gathering: Contemporary Village Politics in Panama*. Austin: University of Texas Press.
Howe, James, Joel Sherzer, and Mac Chapin
  1980 *Cantos y oraciones del congreso Cuna*. Panama City: Editorial Universitaria.
Kramer, Fritz W.
  1970 *Literature among the Cuna Indians*. Etnologiska Studier 30. Göteborg: Göteborgs Etnografiska Museum.
Kungiler, Iguaniginape, comp.
  1997 *Yar burba, anmar burba: Espíritu de tierra, nuestro espíritu*. Panama City: Congreso General de la Cultura Kuna.
Martin, Laura
  1997 "La historia de los huérfanos en casa de los Mochos: Variación y cultura en le cuento de Hansel y Gretel." *Segundo Congreso de Estudios Mayas (Estudios Sociales 58)*, pp. 39–53. Guatemala City: Instituto de Investigaciones Económicos y Sociales, Universidad Rafael Landivar.
McCosker, Sandra Smith
  1974 *The Lullabies of the San Blas Cuna Indians of Panama*. Etnologiska Studier 33. Göteborg: Göteborgs Etnografiska Museum.
Parker, Ann, and Avon Neal
  1977 *Molas: Folk Art of the Cuna Indians*. New York: Barre.

Peñalosa, Fernando
    1996   *El cuento maya popular: Una introducción*. Rancho Palos Verdes, Calif.: Edicones Yax Te'.

Salvador, Mari Lyn
    1978   *Yer dailege: Kuna Women's Art*. Albuquerque: University of New Mexico Press.

Salvador, Mari Lyn, ed.
    1997   *The Art of Being Kuna: Layers of Meaning among the Kuna of Panama*. Los Angeles: UCLA Fowler Museum of Cultural History.

Severi, Carlo, and Ernesto Gomez
    1983   "*Nia ikala*, Los pueblos del camino de la locura. Texto Cuna y traducción española." *Amerindia: Revue d'Ethnolinguistique Amérindienne* 8: 129–179.

Sherzer, Joel
    1983   *Kuna Ways of Speaking: An Ethnographic Perspective*. Austin: University of Texas Press.
    1990   *Verbal Art in San Blas: Kuna Culture through Its Discourse*. Cambridge: Cambridge University Press.
    1995   "'Your Friend Is Peeing Standing Up': Kuna Positional Suffixes in Grammatical, Discourse, Poetic, and Sociocultural Context." In Pam Silberman and Jonathan Loftin, eds., *Salsa II (Proceedings of the Second Annual Symposium about Language and Society – Austin*, 196–211. Austin: University of Texas Department of Linguistics.
    1997   "'Turtle and Jaguar': A Kuna Animal Story in Cultural Context." *Latin American Indian Literatures Journal* 13(2): 1–16.

Taggart, James M.
    1986   "'Hansel and Gretel' in Spain and Mexico." *Journal of American Folklore* 99: 435–460.

Tatar, Maria
    1987   *The Hard Facts of the Grimms' Fairy Tales*. Princeton, N.J.: Princeton University Press.

Thompson, Stith
    1961   *The Types of the Folktale*. Helsinki: Folklore Fellows Communication No. 184.

Urrutia, Anselmo, and Joel Sherzer
    2000   "'The Way of the Coco Counsel' from the Kuna Indians of Panama." In Kay Sammons and Joel Sherzer, eds., *Translating Native American Verbal Art: Ethnopoetics and Ethnography of Speaking*, 141–157.Washington, D.C.: Smithsonian Institution Press.

Wafer, Lionel
    1970 [1699]   *A New Voyage and Description of the Isthmus of America*. New York: Burt Franklin.

Wassen, Henry
    1937   *Some Cuna Indian Animal Stories, with Original Texts*. Etnologiska Studier 4. Göteborg: Göteborgs Etnografiska Museum.

Index

AILLA (Archive of Indigenous Languages of Latin America), 7, 241n1 (chap. 1)
Animals, 3, 14, 61, 193, 237

Blacks, 47
Body position. *See* Positional suffixes

Chants, 3, 191, 213, 214. *See also* Curing and magical chants
Chicha, 2, 3, 84, 147–148, 150–151, 192, 195, 213, 215, 223. *See also* Puberty rites
Conversation, 3. *See also* Quotation
Costa Rica, 241n1 (chap. 2)
Counsel, 83–84, 93, 223, 237
Curing and magical chants, 2, 83, 84, 91, 129–131, 147, 191, 223

Devil, 15, 84–85, 192, 194
Drinking, 3, 148, 150–151, 191–192, 195, 213. *See also* Chicha; Puberty rites

Ecology, 3, 14, 61
European origins of stories, 2, 13–14, 48

Family structure, 3, 14, 47, 130, 194. *See also* Gender; Women

Gathering house, 1–2, 15
Gender, 3, 194–195, 224. *See also* Family structure; Women
Grammar, 5, 60, 84, 93–94, 131–132, 148–149, 192, 214, 223–224
Grandmother, 14–15, 47, 193

Hansel and Gretel, 13
Humor, 1–4, 13, 15, 59–61, 71–72, 93, 132, 191, 193–195, 213–214
Hunting, 61, 129–130

Jaguar, 59

Kuna literature, 1–3, 14
Kuna Yala 1, 238

Linguistics. *See* Grammar
Lullabies, 2, 223–224, 237

Maya, 241n1 (chap. 2)
Message. *See* Moral
Metacommunication, 130, 213, 223, 224
Metaphor, 2, 84, 91, 93, 132, 148, 150, 193, 214
Mexico, 241n1 (chap. 2)
Mola, 1, 7, 148, 151, 215, 223, 224
Moral, 2, 13, 16, 60, 72, 191, 195
Myth, 1, 2

Nahuatl, 241n1 (chap. 2)
Names, 91–92, 94, 130, 193

Onomatopoeia, 6, 15, 48, 72
Oral performance, 1, 4, 15, 47, 62;
    representation of, 4–6, 47
Orthography, 7–8

Parallelism, 2, 61, 84, 92, 130, 149–
    150, 192–193
Plants, 3, 83, 85, 91, 148
Play. *See* Humor
Positional suffixes, 15, 60, 72, 131–
    132, 148–149, 192. *See also*
    Grammar
Puberty rites, 3, 147–148, 191–192,
    213–215. *See also* Chicha

Quotation, 6, 14, 15, 48, 60, 61, 72,
    131, 149, 193

Reflexive speech. *See* Metacommu-
    nication
Repetition. *See* Parallelism
Reported speech/dialogue. *See* Quo-
    tation

Sea, 193–195, 238
Snakes, 2, 129–130
Social structure, 14. *See also* Family
    structure
Spain, 241n1 (chap. 2)
Spirits, 2, 3, 83–84, 91–94, 129–131,
    147–148, 150, 191, 192–193, 213,
    214
Stories, 2, 60, 71, 72

Translation, 1, 4–6, 93, 132, 150, 193
Trickster, 3, 13–15, 59–61, 71
Turtle, 59, 71, 194–195, 242n2 (chap.
    5)

Vocabulary, 6, 84, 93–94, 132, 150–
    151, 193, 214

Women, 3, 14, 47, 213–214, 223,
    224. *See also* Family structure;
    Gender

LaVergne, TN USA
06 August 2010
192356LV00003B/22/P